SICILIAN ∽ AMERICAN
PASTA
99 RECIPES
YOU CAN'T REFUSE
JOHN PENZA & TONY CORSI

illustrated by MIRIAM DOUGENIS

TEN SPEED PRESS
Berkeley, California

Contents

Green Olives
55. Green Olive and Parsley Pesto / 99

Pasta with Meat

Sausage
56. Ziti with Sausage and Broccoli / 102
57. Rigatoni with Sausage and Peppers / 103
58. Rigatoni with Sausage and Cannellini Beans / 104
59. Linguine with Sausage and Tomato Sauce / 105

Chicken
60. Rigatoni with Chicken and Roast Peppers / 107
61. Orzo with Chicken, Pine Nuts, and Mushrooms / 108
62. Linguine with Chicken, Sausage, and Green Olives / 109
63. Spaghetti with Chicken and Rosemary / 110
64. Fettuccine with Chicken Livers / 111

Duck
65. Spaghetti with Duck, Fennel, and Orange / 113
66. Orzo with Duck / 114

Beef
67. Spaghetti with Meat Sauce / 117

Veal
68. Rigatoni with Veal and Mushrooms / 119

Lamb
69. Ground Lamb and Eggplant Lasagna / 120
70. Acini di Pepe with Lamb, Chickpeas, Herbs, and Vegetables / 122

Ham
71. Lasagna with Ham, Cheese, and Spinach / 124
72. Linguine with Prosciutto and Radicchio / 126

Mixed Meats
73. Baked Shells, Sicilian Style, with Pork, Beef, and Veal / 127

Pasta with Fish

Sardines
74. Perciatelli with Sardines and Currants / 130
75. Perciatelli with Sardines and Olives / 132

Clams
76. Linguine with White Clam Sauce / 132

Mussels
77. Mussels Marinara / 134

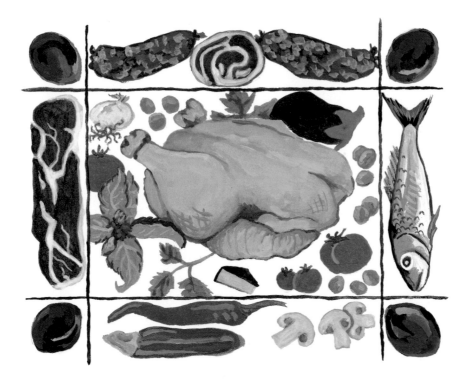

Introduction

As children growing up in Brooklyn, food permeated every aspect of our lives. In the winters, we were fired by big plates of ziti with chicken, black olives, and sausage laced with fennel and hot peppers; the chicken personally delivered fresh-killed every Thursday and Saturday by Uncle Sal, the sausage homemade, from Fiore's meat market on the corner. Summertime brought every little backyard garden in the neighborhood to life with eggplants, zucchini, tomatoes, basil, and Italian parsley surrounding the plastic shrines to Our Lady. From the artichoke hearts that our mothers packed in our lunch boxes to the sumptuous eight-course feasts we had on Sunday afternoons, our ethnic awareness came to us on the end of our forks. We had a hard time imagining that, with all the strange and wonderful animals, vegetables, and fishes that came out of our mothers', aunts', and grandmothers' kitchens dressing our macaroni, we could have been any place but Sicily itself. And, we always joked, the belch that Uncle Mario gave before he had his after-dinner espresso on Sunday afternoons might have been from Mount Etna. . . .

After hearing about the glories that were Rome, one thing many outsiders fail to understand is that, from the beginning of the Middle Ages up until 1861, Italy was composed of many separate city-states. Different regions were politically separate and sometimes hostile to one another. Every region had its own way of cooking and eating, and there was no such thing as "Italian" food.

Sicilian cooking is both different from and similar to that of the rest of Italy, reflecting Sicily's relationship to the mainland. Generally, it is more rustic, but at the same time, as a reflection of the island's long alliance with Naples, the habit is to have pasta at virtually every serious meal. Secure in their *sicilianismo*, Sicilians have no fear of or shame in adapting foods brought from other lands to their own simple style of cooking. And due to its location, the island has had more than enough contact with outside cultures. Situated in the central Mediterranean Sea, Sicily has long been a crossroads for many cultures and civilizations, among them the Greek, Arabic, French, Spanish, and for a brief period, even Austrian. Perhaps the most surprising aspect of this book will be the vast and unsuspected variety to be found in Sicilian cooking. Sicily is truly a melting pot. A world of ingredients has been incorporated into its kitchens, and recipes have been handed down along with family values, jewelry, and weapons.

In the far south of the Italian peninsula, the climate is extreme. The temperature rises; the sun is intense. The tomatoes are redder, the peppers hotter, and the wind blows from the south, hot and dry. This wind, the *scirocco*, which roars across the Mediterranean from the North African desert, carries with it a lean, sunbaked pungency: sweet, spicy, perfumed, and aromatic. These qualities are added to the already fiery and volcanic nature of the Sicilian soil, land long dominated by the tumultuous and repeated mineral-rich eruptions of Mount Etna. These conditions not only heat up the land, but also stimulate passion in the people and their appetites. Undeniably, there is vehemence in Sicilian cooking. Fresh vegetables, herbs, fish, meats, fruits, nuts, and spices are sizzled quickly, almost violently, in crushed hot peppers and olive oil. As the hillsides are rather dry for grazing, and olive groves replace dairies, oil takes the place of butter and cream. Even cheese is not an essential part of most pasta dishes. Sicilian sauces are blends of ingredients that dress one's pasta. In most cases, the ingredients retain their integrity, form, and color and are mixed with the pasta, rather than sitting on top as a garnish.

Although Sicily's geography makes it the solar plexus of the Mediterranean, many times in recorded history the island's sovereignty has been eclipsed. During the eighth century B.C., Sicily was colonized by both the Greeks and the Phoenicians. Five centuries later, the island became the first Roman province. When

8

Rome fell, the Vandals and the Ostrogoths came to Sicily. In 535, it was taken over by the Byzantine Empire and the Greek influence returned. In the ninth century, Muslims from North Africa chased the Byzantines out. It was conquered by the Normans in the 1100s. In 1266, it came under French rule for sixteen years until one night the people of Palermo, spitting mad because some French soldiers had insulted several Sicilian women, slaughtered nearly every one of the French inhabitants of the city. This gruesome event, known as *I Vespri Siciliani* ("Sicilian Vespers"), was celebrated in the opera of the same name by Giuseppe Verdi. The long period of Spanish dominance, along with the Moorish influence, began in 1302 and lasted until the War of the Spanish Succession in 1713. In the truce, Sicily became the property of the duchy of Savoy, which later turned it over to Austria in exchange for Sardinia. In 1734, it fell back into Spanish hands and was ruled by the Bourbon family. It was invaded by Garibaldi in 1860, and the island became part of a united Italy in 1861.

The island's political history has left its mark on Sicily's cuisine, as well as on its language and customs. It is no wonder that such a history has discouraged the Sicilian from trusting in government, for rule was never *by* the Sicilian people. According to the custom of *omerta*, the code of silence, one dishonors oneself and one's family by cooperating with the state. Conversely, the centuries of political turmoil and foreign rule have only served to strengthen the tradition of strong ties within the Sicilian family. Inevitably, with the island overrun by occupying foreigners and traders from every corner of the Mediterranean, there was intermarriage. The proposal of such unions might have met resistance at the outset in Sicilian families, but once one was on the inside of such families, ranks closed around you and the proposition was for life.

It is not, however, the code of silence that makes Sicilian chefs shy about writing recipe books, nor are they loath to give up their secrets. Nothing does their hearts more good than to see people eat. But, what with all the flux and change, there are so many tasty versions and variations of recipes, that it is a more agreeable occupation to cook and eat than it is to write cookbooks.

Our hope is that, from trying the recipes in this book, the reader will get a sense of the style of Sicilian pasta, gain some confidence, *sicilianismo* as we call it, and will not be afraid to be inventive. Although you would be hard-pressed to get a Sicilian to admit it, whatever influences came their way, political, cultural, gastronomical, Sicilians have assimilated them and made them the products of the indisputable Sicilian character. Such adaptability continued on into America, where our grandparents arrived in 1902.

The pasta dishes here are strikingly different from those coming out of northern Italian kitchens. In Sicily, cheese and butter are sparingly used, and cream, never. Serve a cream sauce to a Sicilian and you are in for trouble. The women will ridicule you, and the men—well, let's just say, it can get you a warning. As the story goes, the Duke of Ragusa, a nineteenth-century noble and notable tough guy, was once served a fettuccine Alfredo–type dish at a state dinner in Florence. He openly cursed it as baby food, threw it to the dogs, and stormed out of the dining hall. No doubt there is a tendency among Mediterranean digestions to be intolerant of milk and milk products, but there is also an excitable sensibility of mind that makes the Sicilian imagine the creamy goo as stuff for a milksop kid, something to pacify rather than strengthen. Admittedly, eschewing milk, the Sicilian taste leans toward blood. In the food, one tastes the guts of the earth, the salt of the sea, and the heat of the sun.

The recipes in this book are drawn from the countless dishes we have learned during our travels and in the kitchens of our families. By no means were women the only ones involved in food preparation. Many men in our families were fine cooks, some earning their living as chefs, and a good number of the specialties we've included came from them. In America, as in Italy, there have been marriages outside of the clan. Cooks came into the family who warmed to our way of doing things and who did not hesitate to experiment with ingredients with which they were unfamiliar. To be sure, the kitchen was the scene of many fights about food as well as politics and religion. However, if well prepared, no experiment ever met with resistance at the table. It might sound trite, but we think it's worth reminding you, let your cook's temper fly as it will, the ingredient you should put in everything you cook to make it tasty is a piece of your heart.

It is said that the same temperamental duke had a passion for anything if it was prepared in the special, plain, and delicious, food-loving Sicilian way. He had his chefs importing ingredients from as far away as Japan and relied heavily on Spanish olive oil and eggplants from North Africa. He was criticized by business rivals for his tastes. What was he doing to the Sicilian identity, they wanted to know, eating foods grown on the soil of those who would swallow his country? "I am Sicilian!" the Duke declared, with no lack of self-esteem. "And what I eat is Sicilian because I eat it."

We think the following recipes all make honest, straightforward dishes. Try some. If you don't think so, sit back, have some wine, think, and try again. We're sure you'll see things our way.

Pasta

Directions in most recipes are given for one pound of pasta. This will serve six, four, or two, depending on whether it is offered as an appetizer, a main course, or to macaroni lovers who haven't eaten all day.

We recommend that you buy only imported or premium domestic pasta. The extra money for the high-quality product is insignificant when broken down to a per-serving basis. Likewise, the most expensive is not always the best. You may want to ask the advice of the people in the Italian markets near you. Fresh pasta is good if it's good. Unfortunately, most often it's not. Also, if one wants to be authentic, Sicilians, far from the breadbaskets of the Italian peninsula, rely primarily on the more economical, egg-free, hard macaroni familiar to us.

It is most important to learn to undercook pasta. Package directions are unreliable. Always taste periodically and drain the pot when the pasta is firm, *al dente*, as we say. Toothsome, it should be firm and bite back a little. When in doubt, consider it done. It's better to err on the side of having the pasta stiff and wiry than soft and mushy. Overcooking cannot be fixed, undercooking can. Simply allow the pasta, tossed with the sauce, to sit on the warm stove a little longer. Always reserve some of the water the pasta was cooked in; if needed, it can be added sparingly while you toss the pasta to soften it to perfect tenderness.

Some recipes call for the pasta to be cooked "to the bite." Those with more liquid specifically call for it to be underdone so that it can absorb

the sauce. Getting it to that perfect state, firm and yet tender, takes practice. Until you are experienced, it is best to prepare the sauce first and then the pasta separately so that you can pay complete attention to each. Most sauces benefit from sitting a few minutes while the pasta cooks. Normally, when we enter the kitchen we set the pasta water out on the back burner over low heat, to be brought to a boil at the proper time.

In most recipes, we list the preparation instructions in the list of ingredients. This is because all ingredients should be prepared ahead of time so that the sauce can be made without delays. You shouldn't be chopping parsley or washing basil when it's time to be adding the pepper or garlic to the pan.

We recommend that you use the heating pasta water to rinse the various stirring and chopping utensils, such as the garlic press and the dishes that held the prepared ingredients. Also, the olive oil or water from canned or otherwise packaged ingredients and the stray juices and morsels left on the cutting board can be added to the pasta water. This often makes for a "soupy" version of the sauce on the front burner. The shy, fussy cook might be squeamish about such a procedure, viewing the resultant slick of olive oil from the anchovies, parsley choppings, clam juice, or whatever, as more dishwater than light broth. If so, by all means, that cook should feel free to dispense with this recommendation. But we think pasta cooked in water flavored by the ingredients it will eventually be tossed with acquires an affinity for those same ingredients even before meeting them.

The proportion of pasta to its accompanying ingredients is also a matter of some concern. We do not like our pasta swimming in liquid or other ingredients, but flavored by them. The proportions we advise are to our taste, but a little more or less will do. For appearance's sake, you may want to increase quantities of a star ingredient to use it as a garnish. Then again, if you have a passion for something that you wish to indulge, do it. On the other side of things, a bowl of lightly oiled and subtly seasoned pasta, flavored by hints, rather than chunks, of ingredients, can be one of life's rare treats, every bite a pure-and-simple complex carbohydrate delight. One word of caution: experiments with sauces that produce a lot of watery liquid are suspect. Some of the liquid must be skimmed off and added to the pasta water, saved for use at a later time, or the pasta must be drastically undercooked to accommodate the absorption. Again, as with undercooked pasta, if the dish seems too dry, too plain, you need only add a few drops of olive oil and a tablespoon or two of pasta water to make it work.

Pasta Shapes

All pasta is cut from the same wheat, so why all the shapes? Generally, the shapes correspond to the ingredients in the sauce. Somehow they are supposed to help make getting the food from your plate to your mouth easier, or at least more amusing. Also, many recipes call for a specific pasta because it's traditional. It's just done that way.

Don't hesitate to make substitutions if you can't find the pasta called for, or for any other reason of preference or taste. We recommend, of course, that you use something similar to our recommendations: long pastas for long, short pastas for short.

For example, if you can't find *bucatini* or *perciatelli*, a good, heavy-gauge *linguine* will do perfectly. Or if you can't find *orecchiette, conchiglie* (small shells) will work just as well.

These are the pastas recommended in this book:
acini di pepe: similar to couscous, but larger; *bucatini* cut small
bucatini: long, thick spaghetti, with a thin hole running down the center
capellini: thin spaghetti, also called "angel hair"
cavatelli: short and cupped; a fresh pasta usually made with egg and ricotta cheese
conchiglie: shells
fettuccine: long, flat, wide noodles
fusilli: corkscrews
lasagne: long, flat, very wide noodles
linguine: flat spaghetti
orecchiette: little ears
orzo: rice-shaped, also called *riso*
penne: quills; thin tubes
perciatelli: Neapolitan name for *bucatini*
radiatore: radiators; novelty pasta
ravioli: stuffed squares or circles
rigatoni: ridged larger tubes
rotelli: wheels
spaghetti: the one and only
spaghettini: thin spaghetti
tortellini: bite-sized cheese or meat pies
trenette: long, flat, curly-edged noodles
ziti: medium tubes

Salt and Pepper

We do not list salt as an ingredient in the recipes . However, your pasta water should be salted. How much salt you use is up to you. The right amount varies from dish to dish, from person to person. Obviously, the pasta water in a recipe that calls for anchovies, capers, and black olives needs less salt than the water for a dish in which there are no salty ingredients. Our recommendation is that, unless you are avoiding salt for some reason, you use two tablespoons in six quarts (6L) of water. When you taste the pasta for doneness, also taste for salt and add more if you think it needs it. **We never add salt to our sauces or to cooked pasta, only to the pasta water.**

We include pepper in all recipes and give specific amounts because dishes should have their characteristic spiciness—mild, medium, or hot. We recommend seasoning dishes with crushed red pepper or fresh red and green chilies rather than black pepper. Again, the right amount depends on you. Generally, ¼ teaspoon of dried crushed red pepper per pound (500 g) of pasta will make a dish mildly warm, ½ teaspoon will let you taste the pepper, and ¾ teaspoon or more will make it hot. But this, too, is subjective. We list amounts merely as a guide to give you an idea that the hot flavor is an essential part of the dish.

We do not care so much for black pepper. Red pepper makes one's whole system glow; black seems to burn the mouth. Many claim that there are cardiovascular benefits to eating red pepper. We don't know if this is true, but we like the sound of it because we use more than our share. If black pepper is to be used, it should be the choice of individual diners and added to the dish at the table.

Olive Oil

Always use good quality olive oil. In recipes where there are no animal fats, you can afford to be extra generous. If a dish needs more oil, don't hesitate to increase the amount. It is a fact that a certain amount of fat in the diet is necessary for human happiness, and those who try to skip it entirely, foregoing reasonable amounts, often find themselves unsatisfied, unbalanced, depressed, and bingeing regularly on the much worse beef fats and saturated vegetable oils in hamburgers and french fries. It is cultural propaganda that makes us loathe and love grease so. In the Mediterranean world, a fresh zucchini fried in pure olive oil is considered healthy, a satisfying source of essential oils and calories. We say a good daily dose of olive oil is an acceptable middle ground for those who walk that line between fat-free and fat-bound.

Olives

Many of the recipes call for olives, a staple of the Mediterranean world. We distinguish between green and black olives, and there are several types of each. When we say green olives, we mean large, oil-cured, Sicilian style olives in olive oil and herbs. As for black olives, either the small, oil-cured or large, Greek style olives will work. The different types of olives you will need can be found in most Italian, Greek, or Middle Eastern grocery stores. Never use olives that come from jars or cans unless you have to. And always remove the pits from the olives when serving them with pasta.

*

Cheese

Generally, cheese goes with all meat sauces and many vegetable sauces but not with fish sauces. To enhance the lighter vegetable sauces, serve them with freshly ground Parmesan cheese. For heavier dishes, red sauces, meat ragouts, and so forth, a sharp- flavored Romano-type of cheese (*locatelli* or *pecorino*) is best. As for grated cheese on beans, hot pepper, and garlic, top pasta authorities might disagree, but what is popular may not be proper.

Some recipes call for a dollop or two of fresh ricotta or creamy and tangy goat cheese, perhaps some Greek feta. These are the closest things to cream sauces you will find herein. Mozzarella is used in some baked pasta dishes. There are also some recipes that call for more unusual Italian cheeses such as *ricotta salata*, Asiago, or *caciocavallo*. These can be found in Italian groceries.

*

Herbs

The main herbs used in Italian cooking are basil, parsley, oregano, rosemary, and garlic. These impart a certain essential Italian flavor, taste, and aroma to any sauce or dish in which they are used. We recommend using fresh herbs when possible and have found the following methods excellent for storing fresh basil and parsley.

Basil: In our experience, basil is one of the most fragile herbs. It seems to blacken and become slimy faster than other greens do. To store: Remove the basil leaves from the stems. Wash them thoroughly, then dry them in a towel or salad spinner. The leaves must be very well dried. Place them in a sealed, airtight container and refrigerate. Stored this way, the leaves stay green and keep their integrity for up to a week.

Parsley: We cook for flavor, not decoration. Therefore, let us start by saying that when we say parsley, we mean Italian parsley, which is flat and has distinctive leaves as well as a distinctive taste. Curly parsley may have its place on an hors d'oeuvres tray in the wine and cheese belt, but it can't hold a candle to Italian parsley. That's not to say that we wouldn't use it in an emergency. To prepare: Wash the parsley well, making sure to remove all sand and grit. Try to line the parsley up by the stems so that you can grab them to shake off the excess water. Lay out a double thickness of paper towel, preferably white, place the damp parsley on it, and roll the parsley tightly in the paper towel. Place in a plastic bag and store in the refrigerator. Not only will this method keep the parsley fresh for up to two weeks, but it will also revive limp, wilting parsley.

As for **oregano,** unless you have a garden, the fresh item is hard to come by. It is closely related to marjoram, which is milder in flavor. It takes large quantities of fresh oregano to equal the flavor of just 1 teaspoon of the dried, which is far more intense in flavor.

Thyme, sage, chives, rosemary, and **bay leaf** are called for in many recipes in this book. They can all be used dried or fresh. Unlike oregano, fresh rosemary is far more intense than the dried, so you must adjust the quantities accordingly.

Unless specifically called for, herbs and seasonings should be used to enhance the flavor of a particular dish, never to overpower it. This is especially true in the case of **garlic,** which, while it is essential to Sicilian American cooking, should be used with some discretion. Too heavy a hand with garlic can overpower your taste buds as well as your digestion. We use only fresh garlic and we would never dream of using anything but. We would rather not mention the substitutes, garlic powder and garlic salt, and would *never* use them.

*

Tomatoes

Although tomatoes are thought of as the sine qua non of southern Italian cooking, many of our recipes do without them. Often we add a tomato or two to increase the liquid in a dish, to make it juicy rather than to create a tomato sauce. If you live in a place where fresh tomatoes are available, by all means use them. If canned tomatoes are used, buy the whole, peeled, imported Italian plum tomatoes. The liquid in which they are packed can be a welcome additive to your pasta water.

So when we say
    1 lb (500 g) tomatoes
we mean
    1 lb (500 g) fresh tomatoes or 1 lb (500 g) canned tomatoes without the packing juice.

Two medium-sized fresh tomatoes weigh about a pound (500 grams). This is equivalent to six fresh plum tomatoes or eight from a can.

We always peel fresh tomatoes before we cook them, and although we have seen many cookbooks that instruct you to discard the tomato seeds as well as the juice, we have never found this necessary. In fact, we consider the juice a necessary part of the liquid to be absorbed by the pasta and frequently add tomato to a recipe for this reason alone. But remember, the juicier the sauce, the more undercooked the pasta will have to be to absorb it all.

To peel a tomato, drop it in boiling water for twenty seconds. Remove it from the water and the skin will slip off.

Pesto

Of all the fad foods to have appeared in America in the past twenty-five years, basil pesto is second only to frozen yogurt in popularity. Many people think pesto is confined to the mixture made with basil and pine nuts, a dish originating in Genoa. Throughout Italy, *pesto*, literally "paste," has long been made from any number of different ingredients, usually what was fresh, local, and in season. The recipes are characteristically simple to make, high in fiber, and low in fat. As in America, the Genovese basil pesto recipe enjoyed favor throughout the Italian peninsula, as far south as Sicily, where it joined the repertories of cooks mashing everything from fish heads to crocus flowers in their mortars and pestles.

We have included a good sampling of such sauces in this book: see recipe numbers (1) pesto of cauliflower, (31) artichokes, (36) fennel, (40) mushroom, (44) fava bean, (46) chickpea and eggplant, (55) green olive, and (24) a Sicilian basil pesto.

Utensils

Two pots are needed to make most of the dishes in this book. We recommend a tall, good-quality eight-quart (8L) pot for cooking the pasta and a heavy-duty five-quart (5L) pot with a lid or a heavy frying pan with a lid for the sauce. The lid should fit tightly to seal in the flavors. The sauce pot, if it is made of enamelled cast iron or some other decorative material, might very well be used as a serving dish. A flameproof casserole might also serve very well from stove to table.

After you've drained the pasta, for which you need a colander, return it to the roomy eight-quart pot to toss it thoroughly with the other ingredients. Then turn the mixture into your sauce pot. Because it has been on the stove with the sauce and has a lid, it will keep the food warm. When serving, always dig around the bottom of the pot for "fixings" to top off each serving.

A wooden spoon and a pasta fork are useful for stirring, tossing, and serving.

Pasta with Vegetables
Legumi

First, we will look at a variety of dishes in which the pasta is flavored primarily with vegetables. Many are rustic, easy to prepare, and easy to digest, and it is often these simpler ones that can't be beaten for delectability. Because these recipes generally rely on a few plain ingredients, the quality of the ingredients and the care taken in their preparation make all the difference in the taste or texture.

The area around Etna, in the northeast corner of Sicily, from Taormina to Adrano, is extra fertile due to the presence of volcanic ash in the soil. The vegetables and produce in markets all over the island are beautiful, flavorful, and fresh: healthy broccolis, hearty cauliflowers, deep green leaf vegetables, vine-ripe sweet peppers, juicy tomatoes, firm eggplants and zucchinis, sweet nuts, and all manner of pungent herbs and spices. At home in America, we seek out good vegetable stores and look for what is fresh, what looks best, what is local. It is then that we decide what we are going to eat, not before.

We make no claims for the health benefits of vegetables. However, our Grandaunt Angela lives to be ninety-nine, still cooks for herself, and every night dines on one of a dozen or so basic dishes: macaroni with squash, cauliflower, peas, onions, beans, zucchini, and so forth, always accompanied by a glass of wine. As kids we liked to visit her because she always gave us a glass with dinner. At the same time, we learned to enjoy and cook meatless meals. She would say mystical things such as, "This eggplant is my body, and this vino is my blood."

We understood. If a zucchini is to be your meat, make sure it's not an anemic one. The wine made us understand that food was a sacrament.

Cauliflower
Cavolfiore

Good cauliflower is available in the markets throughout the year. However, it seems best in the fall. Perhaps this is because our family celebrated the arrival of back-to-school days with a medley of pasta dishes using the flowering heads in a variety of ways. The following recipes are our all-time favorites. Choose crisp, white heads. The heavier compact ones with tight florets are more flavorful and have a better texture when they are cooked than those that are rubbery and less dense.

1
Cauliflower Pesto
Linguine al Pesto Cavolfiore

This is simple to make, but not instant. It requires neither food processor nor mortar, but it takes some time to cook the cauliflower. The more peppery you can take it, the better.

1 cauliflower
1 teaspoon crushed red pepper, or more or less, to taste
½ cup (125 ml) olive oil
1 lb (500 g) linguine
grated Parmesan cheese, optional, for the table

Wash the cauliflower and remove the leaves and the base of the stem, leaving the head intact. Place it in salted, cold water in the pot in which you will eventually boil the pasta. Bring to a boil over high heat, then lower the heat to keep the water from boiling over. Cook until very tender, about fifteen minutes, although this depends on the density of the head. The cauliflower should be on the verge of falling apart.

Remove the cauliflower from the pot. Do not discard the water. Separate florets, and chop up the central stem if it is tender enough.

Heat the pepper and oil in a saucepan over medium-high heat. When the oil is hot and the pepper is browning, add the cauliflower. Stir briefly, lower heat, and mash to a paste. Add two or three tablespoons of the water from the pasta pot, stir, cover, and simmer.

Bring the water back to a boil and begin to cook the pasta.

Check the cauliflower now and then as it simmers, adding tablespoons of pasta water, as needed, to keep the simmering cauliflower mash from sticking or burning. Cook pasta until almost tender, drain, and toss with the cauliflower. Let sit on warm range five minutes, stirring occasionally.

Can be served with or without Parmesan cheese.

2
Rigatoni with Cauliflower, Saffron, and Black Olives
Pasta con Cavolfiore

Like many Sicilian dishes, this one is flavored with black olives, capers, and anchovies—the robust essences of the land and the sea. Unlike the seemingly similar eggplant recipe (5), in which the eggplant has a mushy texture, a subtle flavor, and is overwhelmed by the salt and earthiness of the other ingredients, here the cauliflower stands out like a king with its convincing regal qualities—a vegetable with both body and soul.

1 cauliflower
½ cup (125 ml) olive oil
1 clove garlic, crushed
½ teaspoon crushed red pepper
pinch (500 mg) saffron
½ lb (250 g) tomatoes, peeled and chopped
6 anchovies, drained and rinsed
1 tablespoon salt-cured capers
6 oil-cured black olives, pitted and coarsely chopped
1 lb (500 g) rigatoni
grated Parmesan cheese, optional, for the table

Rinse the cauliflower and remove the outer leaves. Fill your pasta pot with cold water, salted to taste. Place the whole cauliflower into it, and set over high heat until the water begins to boil. Lower the heat and simmer five minutes. The cauliflower should be firm, but cooked through. Use a slotted spoon to remove the cauliflower. Don't pour out the water. You will be cooking the rigatoni in it. When the cauliflower is cool enough to handle, cut it into florets, trimming away the tough parts. Some of the florets will be too large. Cut these into bite-sized pieces.

Pour the olive oil into your saucepan. Sauté the garlic and pepper over high heat until the garlic begins to brown. Then add the cauliflower, stirring quickly a few moments to braise on all sides. Be careful not to let it burn. Lower the heat.

Add the saffron, and continue to stir until the cauliflower turns pink. Then add the tomatoes, anchovies, capers, and olives, together with ¼ cup (60 ml) of water from the pasta pot. Cover. Cook over low heat five minutes.

In the meantime, start cooking the rigatoni. When the pasta is tender, drain and toss with the other ingredients.

Again, we feel cheese is optional in this dish. It is an essential part, however, of the following recipe.

3
Cauliflower Ears
Orecchiette con Cavolfiore, Pancetta e Pecorino

Nothing in common with getting batted around the ring here.
This dish gets its name from the orecchiette, small, ear-shaped pasta,
spiked with cheese and reddish gold saffron. They are available in
Italian groceries. If you cannot find them, cavatelli, conchiglie, or any
small shell-shaped pasta will do.

> 1 small to medium cauliflower that will yield 2 cups (375 g)
>   cooked florets
> 2 tablespoons pine nuts
> ½ cup (125 ml) olive oil
> ¼ lb (125 g) pancetta, thickly sliced then diced to ¼ inch (5
>   mm) squares
> generous pinch (1 g) saffron
> ¼ teaspoon crushed red pepper
> 1 lb (500 g) orecchiette
> ¼ cup (30 g) Pecorino Romano cheese, grated

Bring salted water in your pasta pot to a boil. Place the cauliflower
head in it and boil six minutes. Remove the cauliflower from the water
and set aside to cool. Remember to save the water to cook the pasta.

In the meantime, roast the pine nuts in a heavy pan, shaking it over
high heat until they are golden brown. Set them aside.

Put a tablespoon of the olive oil in your sauce pot and cook the *pancetta*
over medium-high heat, about five to seven minutes, until it starts to get
crisp. Remove with a slotted spoon and set aside. Pour off extra fat.

Dissolve the saffron in ¼ cup (60 ml) water from the pasta pot.

Cut the cauliflower into small florets and measure out 2 cups (500 ml).
(Any left over can be saved, refrigerated, or frozen.) Heat the remaining
olive oil with the red pepper in your sauce pot. Add the cauliflower.
Stir-fry over high heat a minute or two. Pour in the saffron water. Mix
thoroughly. Add the bacon and the pine nuts. Mix thoroughly again.
Lower heat. Add a tablespoon or two of the pasta water if the mixture
seems dry. Cover and simmer five minutes. The cauliflower should be
just a bit *al dente*.

Cook the orecchiette in the water in which you've cooked the cauliflower. Reserve ¼ cup (60 ml) water. Drain the pasta and add it to the
pot holding the cauliflower sauce. Toss. Add the cheese a little at a time,
mixing well, and adding a tablespoon or two of the reserved pasta water,
if necessary, to make the mixture smoother.

Eggplant (Aubergine)
Melanzane

In Sicily, there are numerous recipes for pasta with eggplant. We enjoy it in ninety-nine different ways ourselves. Included here are some of our favorites.

In general, eggplants need to be prepared before they are cooked. As members of the nightshade family, they have a bitterness that should be purged. First, peel and cut the eggplant as called for in the recipe. Place it in your colander. Because the eggplant will be draining, place the colander over the sink or some receptacle to catch the water (your empty pasta pot should do nicely). Salt the eggplant pieces generously. Place a dish or bowl that is smaller than the circumference of the colander on top of the eggplant, and put a weight on top of it to press the bitter liquid out of the eggplant. A large can of tomatoes or a brick on a flat plate will work.) Let the eggplant pieces sit an hour, then rinse them under cold water to get rid of excess salt. Press out any additional water by squeezing them between the palms of your hands. If you are weak, put them in a clean hand towel and twist all the water you can from them. This towel method will only work for eggplant cut in cubes, not in rounds. Our grandmother would place the eggplant slices flat on the counter between two kitchen towels and press down on them to squeeze out excess moisture.

Use regular eggplants or the smaller Italian ones if you can find them. (Do not confuse them with the Japanese miniatures!) A good eggplant feels solid, not soft; its skin should be slick, glossy, and unmarked purple.

4
Spaghetti with Fried Eggplant
and Tomato Sauce
Spaghetti Norma

This recipe is made with a simple tomato sauce that uses as its base the
olive oil in which you fry the eggplant. If you would rather the dish
were less oily, you may grill the eggplant in the oven broiler or, better
still, over hot charcoal.

The name is a mystery. Any dish with spaghetti and eggplant can be
called *Norma*. Some sources relate it to Bellini's opera by the same
name, citing the composer's partiality to eggplant. We think it more
likely that spaghetti with eggplant is "normal" spaghetti, something
you might typically eat.

¾ cup (185 ml) olive oil

2 lb (1 kg) eggplant (aubergine), peeled, cut in rounds about
½ inch (1 cm) in width, salted, drained, and wrung of
excess water (see page 24)

1 large clove garlic, pressed or chopped

½ teaspoon crushed red pepper

2 lb (1 kg) tomatoes, peeled and cut in eighths (quarters for
plum tomatoes)

¼ cup (30 g) Italian parsley, finely chopped

30 large basil leaves

½ teaspoon dried oregano

1 lb (500 g) spaghetti

grated Parmesan cheese, for the table

Prepare your ingredients, and when everything is ready, place the oil
in a large skillet over medium-high heat. When the oil is hot, put in the
eggplant slices, gently, one by one. Do not overload, or the oil will cool,
making the eggplant spongey. Do not put in too few slices, either, or the
oil will start to burn. When done on one side, turn and fry the other side.
Remove the slices from the oil when they are golden brown on both
sides, letting excess oil drain back into the pan. Set the cooked slices
aside, keeping them warm as you continue frying the remaining slices.

Use the oil left in the saucepan to make your tomato sauce. Reheat it
if necessary, and add the garlic and red pepper. Before the garlic burns,
add the tomatoes, stir a minute, then add the parsley, basil, and oregano.
Stir until all ingredients are thoroughly mixed. Reduce the heat, cover,
and continue cooking about fifteen minutes until the sauce is smooth.

While the sauce is simmering, cook the spaghetti. Drain when slightly
underdone. Toss with the tomato sauce. Let sit on the stove a few minutes until the pasta absorbs the liquid from the sauce.

(Continued)

After serving pasta in bowls, place several slices of the fried eggplant atop each dish.

Serve with the grated Parmesan cheese at the table.

Variation: For grilled eggplant, cut the eggplant into slices ½ inch (1 cm) thick. Leave the skin on as it will hold the eggplant together. Brush with olive oil and salt and place on a hot grill, or under a hot broiler, a minute or two on each side.

5

Linguine with Eggplant, Black Olives, and Capers

Pasta con Melanzane Siciliano

Here is a relish that's so salty it's sweet. You might want to reduce the salt in the pasta water. This sauce is very strong. A little bit goes a long way.

½ cup (125 ml) olive oil

½ teaspoon crushed red pepper

1 clove garlic, crushed

1 lb (500 g) eggplant (aubergine), peeled, diced ¾ inch (2cm), salted, drained, and wrung of excess water (see page 24)

½ lb (250 g) tomatoes, peeled and chopped

4 anchovies, drained and rinsed

2 tablespoons salted capers

8 oil-cured black olives, pitted and chopped finely

1 lb (500 g) spaghetti

2 tablespoons Italian parsley, finely chopped

grated Parmesan cheese for the table

Heat the oil in your sauce pot and add the pepper and garlic.

Sauté the eggplant over high heat until brown and soft, about five minutes. Add the tomatoes, anchovies, capers, and olives. Sauté briefly a minute or so, then reduce heat, cover, and cook five minutes. The anchovies will melt.

Cook the pasta, drain, and toss with the sauce, and add the parsley.

Serve with grated Parmesan cheese.

Variations: A few slices of roasted red (sweet) pepper may be added for taste and color along with the tomatoes. Or, if you have some cooked broccoli, a small quantity of florets, cut in small pieces, can be added at that time.

6
Cheese Tortellini with Caponata
Tortellini con Caponata

It is worth making an extra quantity of this recipe as it is an excellent cold appetizer or side-dish accompaniment to a main course. Caponata can be made ahead of time and stored. In fact, its flavor is improved by standing. Served with tortellini, it makes a wonderful party dish. Tortellini are small meat- or cheese-filled folded rounds, sometimes fresh, but usually found in the frozen-food section of the market. As with other filled pasta, one pound (500 g) does not usually go far enough to serve four. We suggest two pounds (1 kg) of pasta. Any leftovers will be sought after.

¼ cup (60 ml) plus 2 tablespoons (30 ml) olive oil

1 clove garlic, crushed or finely chopped

2 lb (1 kg) eggplant (aubergine), peeled and cut into ½-inch (1-cm) cubes, salted, drained, and wrung of excess water. (see page 24)

½ teaspoon crushed red pepper or chopped hot chile pepper

½ cup (90 g) chopped onion

1 cup (185 g) chopped celery

8 oil-cured, sun-dried tomatoes, chopped

2 tablespoons pine nuts

6 large green olives, pitted and cut into slivers

2 tablespoons balsamic vinegar

2 tablespoons tomato paste

2 lb (1 kg) cheese tortellini

grated Parmesan cheese, for the table

In your saucepan, heat ¼ cup (60 ml) of the olive oil with the crushed garlic. When it starts to sizzle, add the diced eggplant and sauté over medium heat four minutes, stirring until the eggplant is soft and slightly browned. Remove from the pan with a slotted spoon and set aside.

Add the remaining 2 tablespoons of the oil, red pepper, and onion to the saucepan. Sauté over medium heat, stirring for two minutes. Add the celery, stir two minutes, add the sun-dried tomatoes, pine nuts, and slivered olives, and stir two minutes more.

Lower the heat, add the cooked eggplant, balsamic vinegar, and tomato paste. Mix well, cover, and cook twenty-five to thirty minutes, stirring occasionally. The result should be somewhat homogenized with a relishlike consistency: caponata.

Cook the tortellini as directed, drain, and add the caponata until the pasta is well coated. You can refrigerate any caponata that is left over.

Serve with grated Parmesan cheese.

Variations: Add one or more of the following: capers, currants, white wine, basil leaves, raisins, anchovies, mint, roasted sweet red pepper, oil-cured black olives—anything from zucchini marinated in vinegar to nuts. These should be added when you add the sun-dried tomatoes.

7
Spaghetti with Eggplant and Ricotta
Spaghetti con Melanzane y Ricotta

This dish is cool, sweet, and mild, white and green, perfect for a simple summer supper.

2 cloves garlic, pressed or minced
¼ teaspoon crushed red pepper
½ cup (125 ml) olive oil
2 lb (1 kg) eggplant (aubergine), peeled, diced 1 to 2 inches (2.5 to 5 cm), salted, drained, and wrung of excess water (see page 24)
1 lb (500 g) spaghetti
¼ cup (30 g) Italian parsley, chopped
25 fresh basil leaves
3 tablespoons ricotta
2 tablespoons grated Parmesan cheese

Put the garlic and pepper in the oil in a frying pan over medium heat. Sauté, briefly, about a minute. Then add the eggplant. Sauté, stirring constantly, until the eggplant is lightly browned on all sides, about ten minutes. Cover. Keep warm.

Bring the pasta water to a boil. Cook the spaghetti, drain, and toss with the eggplant over low heat. Add the parsley and basil, then the ricotta and Parmesan, tossing until all ingredients are thoroughly mixed.

8
Rigatoni Ratatouille
Rigatoni Autunnale

This dish shows the French influence. We love to make it at the end of
August and September when the garden is full of fresh vegetables.
Ideally, the vegetables maintain a chunky integrity. As eggplant tends
to become mushy when cooked, we recommend leaving on the skin for
this recipe.

½ cup (125 ml) olive oil

2 cloves garlic, coarsely chopped

1 finger-hot chile pepper, cherry, jalapeño, or a similar
variety, finely chopped (use those seeds!)

1 cup (185 g) red onion, coarsely chopped

1 lb (500 g) eggplant (aubergine), diced 1 inch (2.5 cm),
salted, drained, and wrung of excess water (see page 24)

1 lb (500 g) zucchini (courgette), diced

½ lb (250 g) sweet red pepper, roasted (see page 80), cut into
rigatoni-sized strips

1 lb (500 g) tomatoes, peeled and cut in eighths

25 large basil leaves

½ teaspoon oregano

¼ cup (30 g) Italian parsley

1 lb (500 g) rigatoni

grated Parmesan cheese, for the table

Heat the olive oil in your sauce pot over medium heat. Add the garlic,
chile pepper, and onion and sauté until the onion is soft, about five
minutes.

Raise the heat a bit and add the eggplant. Sauté until golden. Add
the zucchini. Sauté thirty seconds to one minute. Add the red pepper,
tomatoes, basil, oregano, and parsley. Stir. Lower the heat, cover, and
simmer about twenty minutes.

Cook the rigatoni until it is three-quarters done. Drain. Toss with the
vegetables. Let sit on a warm stove for five or ten minutes (be patient)
until the liquid is absorbed, tossing occasionally. Enjoy a glass of wine
while you wait.

Serve with grated cheese at the table.

Zucchini (Courgette)
Zucchini

Zucchini is perhaps the most friendly vegetable. Peel it or not, cook it any way, with anything, and it will be edible. Choose small, deep glossy green, unpocked, firm zucchini, for these are the most sweet, fresh, and tender. By small we mean an inch (2.5 cm) or so in diameter and no more than six or seven inches (15 cm) in length. Ones that have been left on the vine until they are long and fat are no prizewinners in the kitchen.

9
Spaghetti with Fried Zucchini
Spaghetti con Zucchini Fritti

This recipe is like a mother to me. Thank you Gaetana Penzavecchia.
It is the apple pie of southern Italian cooking: plain, delicious, and
economical. It may take you a try or two to get the hang of perfect,
consistent, golden brown zucchini—you cannot leave the range, and
you must turn them vigilantly, constantly—but it's worth the effort.
Few things in this world are as simple, elegant, and satisfying as this
dish, properly prepared.

2 lb (1 kg) zucchini (courgette)
¾ cup (185 ml) olive oil
1 lb (500 g) spaghetti or spaghettini
grated Parmesan cheese, for the table

Peel the zucchini. Cut into rounds about ⅛ inch (2.5 mm) thick. Heat
the olive oil in a frying pan over high heat. The oil should be hot, but
should not smoke or change color. Put the zucchini rounds in a few at a
time at first, being careful not to add so many that the oil cools or so few
that it burns. Turn them regularly, until they are crinkled and golden
brown on both sides. Remove from the oil and place them in a bowl on
the range to keep them warm while you continue cooking the rest.

When the zucchini are fried, pour the remaining oil into a cup and set aside.

Cook the pasta in salted water until tender. Remove 1 cup (250 ml) of the cooking water and set aside. Drain the pasta in a colander and return it to the pot.

Toss the pasta with the zucchini oil. About 4 to 6 tablespoons (60 to 90 ml) will coat a pound of pasta. Add a tablespoon or more of the reserved pasta water as needed.

Place the spaghetti in bowls and garnish with the fried zucchini rounds. Serve with grated Parmesan cheese at the table. The extra olive oil and pasta water may come to the table for those who like their pasta slippery. The leftover olive oil has a delightful "green" taste and might also be used as a base for other recipes.

Variations: This simple dish can be the basis of more complicated ones.

For example, zucchini fried this way are excellent with cheese ravioli. Try getting the smallest ravioli available (36 to 50 count per 1 lb/500 g), round if possible. When using ravioli for this dish, we prepare extra zucchini, at least one round per ravioli if the ravioli are small, two or more if they are large. They seem to disappear quickly.

Another possibility is to use the oil as the basis for the tomato sauce marinara described in recipe (25). Garnish with the fried zucchini rounds.

Or, after frying the zucchini, let the oil cool and use it as the base for the basil pesto (described on page 53). Toss pasta or cheese ravioli with pesto and garnish with fried zucchini.

10
Baked Ziti with Zucchini
Ziti al Forno con Zucchini e Formaggio

In this dish we undercook all the ingredients, as they will be cooked again when they bake in the oven. Because it was somewhat cooked before being put in the oven, as kids we liked to call this dish "half-baked ziti."

¼ cup (60 ml) olive oil

1 clove garlic, minced

⅛ teaspoon crushed red pepper

1 cup (185 g) chopped onion

1½ lb (750 g) zucchini (courgette), peeled and julienned into ziti-sized pieces

1 lb (500 g) tomatoes, peeled and chopped

10 basil leaves

1 tablespoon Italian parsley, chopped

1 teaspoon oregano

1 lb (500 g) ziti

2 tablespoons ricotta

4 oz (125 g) grated mozzarella

2 tablespoons grated Parmesan cheese, plus extra, for the table

Preheat the oven to 350° F (180° C/gas 4).

Heat the oil with the garlic, pepper, and onion. Sauté over high heat five minutes, stirring until the onion becomes translucent.

Add the zucchini. Continue stirring over high heat two minutes. Add the tomato, basil, parsley, and oregano, making sure to mix well. Cover, turn off heat, and set aside.

Meanwhile, cook the ziti. It should be underdone. Drain and return to the pot. Toss with the zucchini-tomato mixture. Slowly add the ricotta, then the mozzarella, tossing gently as you add the cheese so that it is distributed evenly throughout.

Place the mixture in a well-oiled baking dish. Sprinkle the top with the grated Parmesan, cover, and place in the preheated oven twenty-five minutes. Remove the cover and bake another five minutes to brown. Serve with extra grated Parmesan cheese.

Broccoli
Broccoli

Recent information about broccoli shows that this vegetable is high in fiber and rich in beta-carotene. It was always a favorite of Grandaunt Angela, although we doubt she ever thought about dietary fiber or antioxidants.

Here's her method of cooking perfect *al dente* broccoli every time. Remove the lower two or three inches (5 cm) of the stalk and discard. Place the remaining head in your pasta pot in cold, salted water. Put on the range and turn the heat to high. When the water has just about to come to a boil, remove the broccoli. It will be perfectly parboiled, ready to be cut into florets and skinned, and your pasta water will be infused with the robust green vegetable essence.

Let the broccoli cool, then cut the florets off the main stem and into bite-sized pieces. Large florets might have to be halved or quartered. We recommend removing the skin from the stem. To do so, use a paring knife. Cut in anywhere on the edge of the stem, take the skin between the blade and your thumb, and pull. The fibrous outer layer will come off in wide strips. Cut stems into bite-sized pieces.

It makes sense to parboil the entire head of broccoli. Some heads are bigger than others, but generally 1 pound (500 g) of broccoli will yield 2 cups (375 g). If you parboil more broccoli than a recipe calls for, it can be saved for later use in another recipe or eaten as a vegetable. Cook and cut the broccoli as described and put it in a storage container with a squirt of lemon juice to keep it from discoloring. It can be frozen indefinitely.

11
Ziti with Broccoli
Ziti con Broccoli

Here is a very bare broccoli recipe. If you don't believe you are a good cook, or are one who thinks quick pasta for dinner means opening a jar of Aunt Somebody's tomato sauce, this is a good dish with which to start changing your pattern. If the preparation of the broccoli described above seems too complicated, use an equivalent quantity of frozen broccoli, thawed.

¾ cup (185 ml) olive oil

½ teaspoon crushed red pepper

2 large cloves garlic, minced or crushed

3 cups (500 g) broccoli, parboiled and cut into bit-sized
   florets and pieces (see page 35)

2 tablespoons Italian parsley, finely chopped

1 lb (500 g) ziti

grated Parmesan or ricotta cheese, or both, for the table

Put the oil, pepper, and garlic in a pan over high heat until pepper sizzles and garlic begins to brown. Add the broccoli and stir one minute. Add the parsley. Lower the heat, cover, and cook five minutes or so, to desired tenderness. Florets should remain firm.

This dish tends to be dry, as broccoli, one of the vegetables lowest in fat content, can absorb quite a bit of oil. You may have to add a couple of spoonfuls of water from the pasta pot to the broccoli as it cooks.

Cook the ziti. Drain and toss with the broccoli. Serve with grated cheese. In hot weather, we enjoy this dish with a tablespoon or two of ricotta cheese on top of each serving.

36

12

Spaghetti with Broccoli and Anchovies
Sugo di Broccoli e Acciughe

This is also a rather straightforward dish. After being parboiled, the broccoli is mixed with tomato and anchovies and cooked a bit longer. How much longer depends on your taste. In the five-minute range, you still have attractive, meaty florets to toss with your spaghetti. After fifteen minutes or more, it starts to mash down to "cream of broccoli," a salty green pesto. We recommend it both ways, firm or soft, whichever appeals to you. The call for cheese seems to diminish as the broccoli gets pulpier and more like a purée.

To make the dish provocative, drain and rinse the anchovies in the pasta water while you are parboiling the broccoli. We relish it when that hairy little fish-oil taste gets into everything.

¾ teaspoon crushed red pepper

2 cloves garlic, crushed or finely chopped

¾ cup (185 ml) olive oil

2 cups (375 g) broccoli, parboiled and cut into bite-sized florets and pieces (see page 35)

½ lb (250 g) tomatoes, peeled and chopped

12 anchovies, drained and rinsed

1 lb (500 g) spaghetti

grated Parmesan cheese, for the table

Heat the pepper and the garlic in the oil. While they are hot, add the broccoli. Stir over medium heat for about one minute to coat the broccoli with the hot oil. Then add the tomatoes and anchovies. Stir another minute, cover, lower heat, and cook to desired tenderness.

Cook the spaghetti. Drain and toss with the sauce.

Serve with grated Parmesan cheese.

13

Radiatore with Broccoli, Potatoes, and Peppers
Pasta in Bocca al Lupo

This idiomatic way of saying "Good luck" in Italian, literally, "in the mouth of the wolf," inspired the name of Grandma's New Year's pasta. She believed it would mollify the *mal'occhio*. We thought she was talking about Mr. Bocciagaloupe, our idea of the bogeyman. We still get a good laugh when we recall her bruised pronunciation of *Ingalise*, even though we realize that our Italian is probably more broken than her *Americanese*.

This is a kind of vegetarian witch's brew.

Radiatore is a radiator-shaped novelty pasta. If you cannot find this pasta, use fusilli.

2 cloves garlic, thinly sliced

¼ teaspoon crushed red pepper

½ cup (125 ml) olive oil

½ lb (250 g) sweet red pepper, sliced lengthwise into strips ¼ inch (5 mm) wide

¼ cup (30 g) Italian parsley, chopped

1 lb (500 g) radiatore

1½ cups (¾ lb/ 280 g) potatoes, peeled and diced

2 cups (375 g) broccoli, parboiled and cut into small florets; stems peeled and diced (see page 35)

grated Parmesan cheese, for the table

Sauté the garlic and pepper flakes in the olive oil over high heat. When the pepper and garlic are sizzling, add the red pepper slices, stir briefly, lower the heat to medium, cover, and cook another five minutes over medium heat, stirring occasionally to insure even cooking. Add the parsley, turn off heat, and let sit on a warm range.

In this recipe it is important to know how long the pasta will cook, because you will be adding the potato and broccoli to the boiling pasta for the last minutes of cooking, and you want the pasta and the vegetables to be done at the same time. Remember, adding cold ingredients to the pot slows down cooking time. If you want the pasta *al dente*, figure on cooking it about eight or nine minutes altogether.

Place the pasta in boiling water. After two minutes, add the cubed potatoes and cook three minutes, then add the broccoli and cook three minutes more. The broccoli should be firm and the potatoes tender. If the pasta is not ready, cook the extra minute. It shouldn't make the broccoli too soft.

Drain the pasta (along with the potatoes and broccoli) and mix with the pepper, parsley, and oil in the sauce pot.

Serve with the grated cheese.

14
Cavatelli with Broccoli and Zucchini
Cavatelli Verdure

This dish is fresh, simple, green, friendly, and delicious.
Cavatelli are short concave pasta, like shells, made with eggs and fresh
ricotta cheese. They are available, usually frozen, in Italian groceries
and in many supermarkets next to the frozen ravioli. To be traditional,
the ingredients should read, "flour, water, eggs, ricotta cheese."
The following recipe would be a main course for six.

> ½ cup (125 ml) olive oil
>
> ¾ teaspoon crushed red pepper
>
> 3 cloves garlic, minced
>
> 1 lb (500 g) zucchini (courgette), cut into rounds ¼ inch (5 mm) thick
>
> 3 cups (500 g) broccoli, parboiled and cut into bite-sized florets and pieces (see page 35)
>
> ¼ cup (30 g) Italian parsley, chopped
>
> 20 large basil leaves
>
> 2 lb (1 kg) cavatelli
>
> ¼ lb (125 g) Parmesan cheese, coarsely grated

Place the olive oil in your saucepan with the pepper and garlic over
high heat. Add the zucchini, sauté two minutes. Add the broccoli. Sauté
one minute. Add the parsley and basil. Stir and mix well. Lower the
heat, cover, and cook another four to five minutes. The florets should
stay firm.

Preheat the broiler (grill).

Cook the cavatelli, drain, and toss with the vegetables. Add half the
cheese and mix thoroughly.

Oil a large baking dish. Turn the mixture into it. Spread the remaining
cheese on the top and place under the broiler for three minutes or so (or
for UK and other readers, about five minutes under a medium-high grill),
until the top browns. Serve immediately.

Greens
Verdure

We enjoy a variety of leafy greens, many of which have a subtly bitter taste. Escarole, broccoli rabe, arugula, and spinach are all excellent prepared *stufato*, that is, quickly braised in a pot over high heat with olive oil, crushed red pepper, and sometimes garlic. Though they can be eaten plain as a vegetable, greens are also a quick, delicious, and healthy topping for a plate of pasta. Because of their simplicity, we especially enjoy them on cheese ravioli.

Broccoli Rabe
Rapine

Once upon time, in the not too distant past, broccoli rabe was not widely available. Now, because of the taste and versatility of this somewhat bitter, tangy cousin of the broccoli, it can be found in many ordinary supermarkets.

Some books will tell you to blanche it with boiling water before sautéing to remove some of the bitterness, but we do not think this is necessary. However, we have noticed that letting it sit on the stove after cooking can increase its bitterness.

15
Cheese Ravioli with Broccoli Rabe

Cheese ravioli are widely available. We recommend smaller ravioli, 36 to 48 per pound (500 g), with this dish. Overall, they will have less cheese and more pasta.

Please note, the recipe calls for 2 pounds (1 kg) of ravioli. This may be too much for four people, but we've noticed people eat more when they have stuffed pasta.

    1½ lb (750 g) broccoli rabe

    ½ teaspoon crushed red pepper

    ⅓ cup (85 ml) olive oil

    2 lb (1 kg) cheese ravioli

    2 cloves garlic, minced or crushed (optional)

    ¼ teaspoon ground nutmeg (optional)

    grated Parmesan cheese, for the table

Trim the bottom inch (2.5 cm) or so from the stems of the broccoli rabe. Remove woody stems. Wash thoroughly and shake off the excess moisture or dry on paper towels. Cut the remaining parts into pieces 1 inch (2.5 cm) long.

Heat the pepper in the oil in the sauce pot. If using garlic, put it in now. When the oil is sizzling hot, add the broccoli rabe and stir over high heat until its bulk reduces. If using nutmeg, add it to the broccoli rabe at this time and stir well.

Cover and let simmer over low heat five minutes, or until the thicker stems are cooked.

Cook the ravioli. Drain and toss with broccoli rabe.

Serve with grated Parmesan cheese at the table.

Variations: For variety, the above recipe can be made with escarole, arugula, or spinach, prepared the same way.

Spinach
Spinachi

In hot, dry Sicily, spinach is not that easy to grow, yet it is enjoyed whenever it is available. Here we can always find it fresh, and we have it often, *stufato,* by itself, or with pasta.

16
Rigatoni with Spinach and Cauliflower Oreganata
Rigatoni al'Angie

While Grandaunt Angela would eat no fat, her long-time companion "Uncle" Frank would eat no lean. Due to their different eating habits, they did not often dine together. Except, of course, on Fridays. Uncle Frank would always show up for Angela's vegetarian pasta. He was not religious, but he was very superstitious.

Both Angela, close to the century mark, and Frank, over it, had fond memories of this dish. "Pasture food," Frank recalled and smiled, "but what friggin' Friday nights!"

> 3 to 4 slices bread, to yield 1 cup 4 oz (120 g) croutons
> 2 tablespoons pine nuts
> 1 tablespoon salt-cured capers
> 2 teaspoons dried oregano
> ½ cup (125 ml) plus 2 tablespoons (30 ml) olive oil
> ½ teaspoon crushed red pepper
> 2 cloves garlic, crushed or finely chopped
> 2 tablespoons (30 ml) lemon juice
> ¾ lb (375 g) spinach, stems removed and coarsely chopped
> ½ lb (250 g) endive, sliced into rounds ½-inch (1 cm) thick
> 2 cups (375 g) cauliflower, parboiled, and cut into bite-sized pieces (see page 22)
> 1 lb (500 g) rigatoni

To make the croutons, toast the bread and dice ½ inch (1 cm). Place in a bowl with the pine nuts, capers, and the oregano. Mix well.

Put the 2 tablespoons (30 ml) of olive oil in a large saucepan with ¼ teaspoon of the red pepper and 1 clove of garlic over high heat. When it is sizzling hot, add the crouton mixture, stirring constantly. Add the lemon juice, 1 tablespoon at a time (this will sizzle), and continue stirring. This should take four to five minutes. Remove the croutons from the pan and set aside on the warm stove.

In that same pan, over high heat, place the remaining ½ cup (125 ml) of olive oil, and the rest of the garlic and red pepper. When the oil is hot, add the spinach and endive a little at a time and cook down. Add the cauliflower. Sauté over medium-high heat, stirring constantly until the ingredients are well mixed and coated with the oil, two or three minutes. Lower the heat, cover, and cook five minutes.

Cook the rigatoni, drain, and toss with the vegetables and the crouton–pine nut mixture until all is evenly distributed. Serve immediately.

17

Linguine with Spinach, Sopressata, and Hard-Boiled Eggs

Linguine Vespri Siciliani

In Sicily, hard-boiled eggs wrapped in salami and spinach *stufato* are traditional Easter appetizers going back to Roman times. The poet Virgil mentions it. The tradition of eating this combination with pasta has its origins in the massacre of the French on Easter Monday in 1282. The immediate cause of the riot was wiseguy remarks made by French soldiers to some Sicilian women going to church for vespers. But, in truth, the Sicilians were just looking for an excuse. What seemed like a spontaneous uprising was actually plotted a day earlier, on Easter Sunday. Conspirators, deeply involved in discussions of strategy and weapon checks, didn't have time for a two-course dinner and simply tossed their antipasto on top of their macaroni.
Sopressata is an Italian country-style salami which can be obtained in an Italian meat market and is available in either sweet or hot varieties. We prefer the hot. You might want to try this with both kinds.

> 1 lb (500 g) linguine
> ½ cup (125 ml) olive oil
> ¼ teaspoon crushed red pepper
> ¾ lb (375 g) fresh spinach, stems removed and coarsely chopped
> ¼ lb (125 g) sopressata, thickly sliced then diced ¼ inch (5 mm)
> 2 hard-boiled eggs, chopped
> grated Parmesan cheese, for the table

Have the ingredients prepared and the pasta water at a boil.
Add the pasta to the boiling water.
Heat the oil with the red pepper in a heavy pot. When sizzling, add the spinach, a large handful at a time, stirring constantly to cook down. This should take one to two minutes. Add the sopressata, stirring to mix well, and continue cooking thirty seconds to one minute. Turn off the burner. Add the chopped egg. Cover and keep warm while the pasta finishes cooking.
Drain pasta and toss with the other ingredients. Serve with grated Parmesan cheese.

18
Baked Ziti with Spinach and Ricotta
Ziti al Forno con Spinach

½ cup (125 ml) olive oil
½ teaspoon crushed red pepper
¾ lb (375 g) spinach, stems removed and coarsely chopped
1 lb (500 g) ziti
½ lb (250 g) ricotta cheese
¼ cup (30 g) grated Parmesan cheese

Macaroni and Cheese

Preheat the oven to 375° F (190° C/gas 5).

Heat the oil in a saucepan with the red pepper. When the oil is very hot, add the spinach and stir constantly over high heat a minute or two. You want the spinach to wilt down, not cook completely.

Meanwhile, boil the ziti. Since you are going to bake it, the pasta should be quite *al dente*, half-cooked, like the spinach. Drain the ziti, return it to the empty pasta pot, add the spinach, and mix well. Add the ricotta and mix thoroughly.

Place the ziti-spinach-ricotta mixture in a large, oiled baking dish. Sprinkle the Parmesan cheese on top. Cover and place in the oven twenty minutes. Uncover and bake an additional five minutes, or place under the broiler (grill) for a minute to lightly brown the top.

Variations: If you are a cheese lover, add more cheese. Extra ricotta, grated mozzarella, or grated provolone cheese is good in this old favorite.

Arugula
Rucola

Also called rocket lettuce, arugula is a nutty, tasty green, now available in markets year-round.

19
Linguine with Arugula, Tomato, and Pancetta
Linguine Baroccino

Spaghetti with BLT, but Hold the Mayo

⅓ cup (85 ml) olive oil

¼ lb (125 g) pancetta, thickly sliced then diced ¼ inch (5 mm)

½ teaspoon crushed red pepper

¾ lb (375 g) arugula, coarsely chopped

1 lb (500 g) tomatoes, peeled and chopped

1 lb (500 g) linguine

grated Parmesan cheese, for the table.

Put 1 teaspoon (5 ml) of the olive oil in a pan over medium-high heat, and cook the diced pancetta. Stir constantly. The pancetta bits should become brown and crunchy. This will take about five to ten minutes. Remove the pancetta with a slotted spoon, set aside, and discard the bacon fat.

Add the remaining oil and the red pepper to your saucepan over high heat. When the oil is hot, add the arugula and the tomatoes, stirring constantly until the arugula is wilted and the tomatoes are giving up their juice. Add the bacon bits, lower the heat, cover, and keep warm.

Undercook the pasta. Drain and toss with the "bacon, lettuce, and tomato." Let sit several minutes before serving so that it can absorb all the liquid.

Serve with grated Parmesan cheese.

20
Trenette with Nine-Herb Sauce
Pasta Alla Notte Solstizio d'Estate

There's something fanciful about this recipe, perhaps because we always make it around that magic time of year at the end of June, when the days are the longest, the nights the shortest, and the herbs and spices are young and fresh. To flesh out this dish, we put the herbs in a bed of watercress and arugula. The result is a rich, fragrant, woodsy, savory green sauce. If the mint and parsley are not fresh, they should be omitted. In a pinch, the remaining herbs can be gotten from a jar. Do spend some time at the chopping board, though. The fineness of the minced greens is what gives this recipe its character.
Trenette is a long, flat pasta, similar to fettuccine, but with a curly edge.

1 cup (250 ml) white wine
¼ cup (30 g) Italian parsley
4 sage leaves, (1 teaspoon dried)
2 teaspoons fresh thyme or 1 teaspoon dried
6 to 8 basil leaves
1 tablespoon rosemary leaves, fresh or dried
6 to 8 mint leaves
1 teaspoon dried oregano
2 bay leaves, whole
1 clove garlic, pressed or minced
½ cup (125 ml) olive oil
1 bunch watercress, stems removed and finely chopped to yield 1 cup (125 g)
1 bunch arugula, finely chopped to yield 1 cup (125 g)
1 lb (500 g) trenette or fettuccine
½ cup (60 g) walnuts, finely chopped

Pour the wine into a large mixing bowl. Chop the parsley, sage, thyme, basil, rosemary, and mint as finely as you can. Add them to the wine with the oregano, bay leaves, and garlic and marinate an hour or longer.

Heat the olive oil in your sauce pot on high. When it is hot, add the mashed watercress and arugula. Stir for one minute, until soft and reduced. Add the herbs and wine. Stir. Lower the heat, cover, and simmer twenty minutes. Remove the bay leaves. Add the walnuts.

Meanwhile, cook the trenette. When it is still underdone enough to absorb the liquid left in the sauce, drain and toss with the wine and herb mixture. Let sit on a warm stove, stirring occasionally, heating if necessary, over a low flame, until the underdone pasta is cooked by soaking up the stimulating spicy juices.

21

Rigatoni with Radicchio, Arugula, Endive, and Provolone, Ricotta Salata, Parmesan, and Caciocavallo Cheeses

Rigatoni con Insalata Tricolore e Quattro Formaggi

Red, white, and green are the three colors of the Italian flag. If you find green and red chile peppers, they mix well with the garlic to provide an additional three-color effect. Three times three can be achieved if you can get tricolore rigatoni (white wheat, spinach, and tomato). The sweetness of the cheese overpowers the bitterness of the radicchio, but that biting flavor remains a subtle, savory bass note.
Note that the recipe calls for ricotta salata. This is not the same as fresh ricotta. You will have to go to a cheese specialty shop or Italian grocery store. While you are there, you might be able to find caciocavallo cheese. But this Sicilian sheep-milk cheese is not that readily available, even in Italian groceries. If you cannot find it, we recommend substituting Asiago cheese or using some provolone or extra ricotta salata and Parmesan. There will probably be cheese left over from the amounts given in the recipe. This blend of grated cheese can be used to good effect in soups or salads or on appropriate pasta dishes.

¼ lb (125 g) ricotta salata, grated or finely crumbled
¼ lb (125 g) provolone, finely grated
2 oz (60 g) grated Parmesan cheese
¼ lb (125 g) grated caciocavallo or Asiago
1 lb (500 g) rigatoni
¾ cup (185 ml) olive oil
green and red chile peppers, finely chopped with seeds to
    taste, or ½ teaspoon crushed red pepper
1 large clove garlic, pressed or minced
1 bunch arugula, coarsely chopped
1 head radicchio (6 oz/185 g), finely chopped
2 heads endive, cut into rounds ¼ inch (5 mm) thick

Combine all four grated or crumbled cheeses in a bowl, mixing well.
Bring the pasta water to a boil, and throw in the rigatoni.
Put the oil, peppers, and garlic into the sauce pot and heat over a high flame. When the oil is sizzling hot, add the arugula, radicchio, and endive. Stir over high heat to cook down, one to three minutes, adding a tablespoon or two of pasta water if the mixture seems too dry. Keep cov-

ered over very low heat to keep warm, stirring occasionally, while the pasta continues to cook.

When the rigatoni is done, drain and toss with the arugula, radicchio, and endive mixture. Add a ¼ lb (125 g) of the grated cheese mixture slowly, stirring as you do to insure even distribution.

Serve with remaining grated cheese mixture at the table for those who want to add more.

Escarole
Scarola

Escarole is a long-leafed, lettucelike vegetable in the chicory and endive family, though less bitter. When braised in a pot with hot olive oil, it also makes an excellent side dish.

22
Tortellini with Escarole
Tortellini con Scarola

Here is a simple dish that makes an excellent starter. Note: The recipe is writen to produce a main course that feeds four and calls for 2 pounds (1 kg) of tortellini. Again, filled pastas do not go as far as all-dough pastas in satisfying appetites, at least for big eaters like us. We prefer cheese tortellini, but if you fancy meat or chicken, they will do fine.

> ½ teaspoon crushed red pepper
> 2 cloves garlic, pressed or finely chopped
> ½ cup (125 ml) olive oil
> 2 lb (1 kg) escarole, outer leaves removed, finely sliced 1 inch (2.5 cm)
> 2 lb (1 kg) tortellini
> grated Parmesan cheese, for the table

Heat the pepper and garlic in the oil in a saucepan. When the garlic begins to brown, add the escarole a handful at a time. Sauté over high heat two minutes, or until the bulk of it reduces. Lower heat, cover, and cook fifteen minutes, stirring occasionally.

Cook the tortellini according to package directions. Drain and toss with the escarole.

Serve with grated cheese.

Basil
Basilica

Largely thanks to the following dish, basil, once a fad food, now a staple, is widely available in markets. More than just an herb, it's a fresh vegetable, and the fresher the better. Raise your own. It's easy to grow in the garden or as a houseplant. (See the Introduction for tips on storing these easily bruised, delicate, aromatic leaves.)

 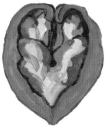 

Basil Pesto
Pesto al Basilica

This sauce, an old standby, is welcome with many pastas. Our version adds parsley to balance the effect of the raw garlic. We recommend less cheese in the pesto than in most recipes, allowing everyone to add more at the table, as they prefer.

basil, (about 80 large leaves)
¼ cup (30 g) Italian parsley
2 tablespoons pine nuts (walnuts or cashews may be substituted)
2 cloves garlic
2 tablespoons grated Parmesan or pecorino cheese
½ teaspoon crushed red pepper
⅔ cup (170 ml) olive oil
grated Parmesan cheese, for the table

Place all the ingredients except the olive oil and extra Parmesan cheese into a blender or food processor. Blend at high speed, gradually adding the olive oil in a thin stream until the ingredients are smooth. The mixture should be liquid enough to coat the pasta easily. If it seems too thick, add an extra tablespoon of olive oil. Transfer the pesto to a bowl and keep in a warm place until ready to use. Pesto that has been refrigerated should be warmed in a low oven or gently heated by placing the container of pesto in a pan of water on top of the stove.

23
Lasagna with Basil Pesto
Lasagna al Pesto Basilica

The following recipe, Grandaunt Angela's most complicated vegetarian accomplishment, is as far from the typical southern Italian-style baked lasagna (dense with cheese, ground beef or sausage, and thick tomato sauce) as you can travel.

2 lb (1 kg) zucchini (courgette)
¾ cup (185 ml) olive oil, plus 1 tablespoon (15 ml)
1 cup (250 ml) basil pesto (see previous page)
1 egg, beaten
1 lb (500 g) fresh ricotta
½ teaspoon grated nutmeg
black pepper, to taste
1 lb (500 g) lasagna
½ lb (250 g) grated mozzarella
¼ cup (30 g) grated Parmesan cheese

Slice then fry the zucchini in the olive oil (see page 32) and set aside. Use the oil in which you fried the zucchini to make the pesto. You will need ⅔ cup (170 ml). Add fresh olive oil if there is not enough.

Make the basil pesto according to the recipe and set aside.

Combine the egg, ricotta cheese, and nutmeg in a bowl. Season to taste with black pepper. Mix thoroughly.

Preheat the oven to 350° F (180° C/gas 4).

Add a tablespoon of olive oil to the pasta water to keep the lasagna from sticking. Boil the lasagna until it becomes just flexible enough to work with, about four to five minutes. Add cold water to the pot to stop the cooking. Drain the noodles and return them to the pot. Add the pesto to the pot and mix thoroughly, making sure to coat the noodles evenly.

Lightly coat the bottom of a baking dish measuring 8 by 10 by 3 inches (20 by 25 by 7 cm) with olive oil. Lay down a foundation of one third of the noodles, overlapping and going up the sides of the pan.

Use a metal spoon dipped in cold water to spread half of the ricotta cheese mixture evenly on the bottom layer of noodles. Sprinkle half of the grated mozzarella on top of the ricotta. Then add half the fried zucchini slices.

Build another layer of noodles, cheese, and vegetables, using the other halves of the ricotta mix, the grated mozzarella, and the zucchini slices.

Top with the third and last layer of noodles, making sure to overlap well. Now spoon any remaining basil pesto left in the pot on top of the lasagna. Sprinkle the grated Parmesan cheese over the pesto.

Cover well and bake thirty-five minutes. Remove the cover and bake another ten minutes. Remove the lasagna from the oven and let it settle ten to fifteen minutes before serving.

Variations: Basil pesto can be used in any of the following ways with pasta:

Using spaghetti or linguine, cook the pasta, drain, and mix with the pesto sauce, making sure that every strand is well coated. A tablespoon or two of reserved pasta water will help the mixing. Serve with grated Parmesan cheese.

Optional: One medium cooked and diced potato may be added to the blender. This will give the pesto an added creaminess without the cream.

*

Add one medium potato, diced ½ inch (1 cm), to the pasta water immediately after you add the pasta. Add ¼ lb (125 g) of French string beans to the pasta water for the last three minutes of cooking. Time it so that the potatoes and beans are done when you drain the pasta. Toss it all with the pesto.

*

Best of all, and highly recommended, fry zucchini and make basil pesto with the oil left over. Toss small cheese ravioli with the pesto and garnish each serving with the fried zucchini. See page 32 for making fried zucchini. This is also good with spaghetti.

24
Tomato, Basil, and Almond Pesto
Pesto Trapanese

This age-old, low-fat recipe is from the Trapani region in Sicily. This dish was reported to be a favorite of Angelo Siciliano, a.k.a. Charles Atlas, famous strongman. He ate this almost daily when he was on vacation from his burdensome bulk-building diet of steak pizziaola and egg fritatas and claimed it kept him from cramping up from the excessive amounts of protein he was forced to consume to fill out his overworked muscles. Ninety-seven-pound weaklings notwithstanding, we swear by this dish for energy.

basil (about 80 large leaves)
1 lb (500 g) tomatoes, peeled and chopped
¾ cup (90 g) blanched almonds
2 cloves garlic, peeled
¼ cup (30 g) Italian parsley leaves
¼ teaspoon hot red pepper, preferably fresh
½ cup (125 ml) olive oil
1 lb (500 g) linguine

Place all the ingredients, except the pasta, in a blender or food processor on high speed until they are well mixed. Place in a bowl and keep warm until you are ready to toss it with the cooked linguine. Bring the pasta water to a boil. Add the linguine and cook until *al dente*. Drain and toss with the pesto.

Tomato
Pomodoro

Tomatoes are a mainstay of southern Italian cooking. Below, we give the recipe for basic tomato sauce, which is not difficult and is well worth the effort. As we have already stated in our introductory notes on tomatoes, start with fresh, whole, red-ripe tomatoes or plum tomatoes whenever possible. If they are unavailable and you must use canned, we recommend using imported peeled Italian plum tomatoes. The Italian plums are plump and juicy. (If using fresh tomatoes, refer to page 16 for their preparation.)

In the past decade, sun-dried tomatoes have become popular all over the world, and in this section we have included a couple of recipes which call for them specifically.

25
Spaghetti with Tomato Sauce
Pasta alla Marinara

This is a basic tomato sauce recipe to which anything can be added. It can be served with any type of long pasta, from vermicelli to perciatelli.

Certainly, *alla marinara* means "seaman's style," referring to sailors and fishermen, and because this basic recipe is so commonly made with clams, mussels, squid, and so forth, it has acquired an association with seafood. However, this is just a basic pizza sauce and goes well by itself or with vegetables, meat, fish, or baked on the tasty Italian bread, focaccia, with cheese.

If using fresh tomatoes, make sure that they are ripe and juicy (see page 16). It they are out of season, it is better to use good-quality canned tomatoes rather than the pale, cardboard-tasting fresh ones available in most markets.

> 2 lb (1 kg) tomatoes, peeled and chopped in eighths
> (quartered, for plum tomatoes)
> ¼ cup (30 g) Italian parsley, finely chopped
> 30 large basil leaves
> 1 teaspoon dried oregano
> ½ cup (125 ml) olive oil
> ½ teaspoon crushed red pepper
> 2 cloves garlic, pressed or minced
> 1 lb (500 g) spaghetti, linguine, or any long pasta
> grated Parmesan cheese, for the table

Mix the tomatoes, parsley, basil, and oregano in a bowl.

Put the oil in your sauce pot with the pepper flakes and the crushed garlic. Heat over a high flame. When the garlic begins to brown and the pepper flakes get snappy, add the tomato mixture. It should sizzle. Stir about one minute until all ingredients are thoroughly mixed and tomatoes are beginning to give up their juice.

Reduce the heat, cover, and continue cooking, several minutes if you like firm tomatoes, fifteen minutes or longer if you like a smooth sauce.

Cook the pasta. Drain when slightly underdone. Toss with the sauce. Allow it to sit on a warm stove five minutes or so, or until the liquid is absorbed. Serve with grated Parmesan cheese.

Note: If you like a thicker sauce, something you can ladle out on top of your spaghetti, add a 6-oz (170-g) can of tomato paste to the above recipe. Stir it in after you reduce the heat, and let it simmer with the sauce until thickened.

26
Spaghetti with Sun-Dried Tomatoes and Goat Cheese
Pasta Caprese

This is delightful and easy to prepare, perfect for a hot summer evening. Since Sicilian goat cheese is not readily available, any good chèvre will do nicely. We are partial to Montrachet.

¼ cup (60 ml) olive oil

½ lb (250 g) tomatoes, peeled and chopped into small pieces

5½ oz (160 g) goat cheese, crumbled

¼ lb (125 g) oil-cured sun-dried tomatoes, coarsely chopped, with the oil

1 tablespoon Italian parsley, finely chopped

30 large basil leaves

2 oz (60 g) prosciutto (or less—don't ham it up), fat trimmed, thinly sliced, and cut into thumbnail-sized pieces

black pepper, to taste

1 lb (500 g) spaghetti

Have all the ingredients prepared. Cook the spaghetti until tender. Drain. Save ½ cup (125 ml) of the pasta water. Transfer the spaghetti back to the pot in which it was cooked.

Then, on a warm stove, mix the ingredients in the following order: olive oil, fresh tomatoes, and goat cheese (if the pasta is dry and the cheese won't "work" or sticks together in lumps, add the reserved pasta water a tablespoon at a time to facilitate the mixing).

Now, add the sun-dried tomatoes, parsley, basil, prosciutto, and pepper, tossing until all ingredients are thoroughly mixed.

Note: The basil will probably wilt considerably in the heat of the pasta. A few additional fresh, green leaves as a garnish will make this dish look as good as it tastes.

27

Bucatini with Tomato and Purple Onions
Bucatini alla Nicosia

Bucatini, or *perciatelli* as it is sometimes called, is a long spaghetti-shaped pasta. Different from spaghetti, it is thicker and has a hole running down the length of the center, rather like a thin straw. With all the extra surface, it is very good for soaking up all kinds of sauce, as it gets coated inside and out. While *bucatini* is the traditional pasta to use in this recipe, if you do not live near an Italian store where the more unusual pastas are available, spaghetti can be substituted with little loss of effect; however, make sure it is the thickest spaghetti you can find.

Pancetta is Italian bacon. It is cured in salt and spices rather than smoked. Again, if you are no stickler for authenticity, you might use ordinary bacon.

¼ cup (60 ml) olive oil

¼ lb (125 g) pancetta, thickly sliced, then diced ¼ inch (5 mm)

1 teaspoon crushed red pepper

½ lb (250 g) purple onion, chopped

2 lb (1 kg) tomatoes, peeled and chopped

1 lb (500 g) bucatini or perciatelli

grated pecorino or locatelli cheese, for the table

Use 1 tablespoon (15 ml) of the olive oil and cook the pancetta over medium-high heat about five to ten minutes, stirring constantly, until the pieces are crisp. Pour off any excess fat. Then add the remaining olive oil, the pepper, and onion. Continue sautéing until the onion is soft, another five minutes. Add the tomatoes. Sauté one more minute. Lower the heat, cover, and simmer twenty minutes, stirring occasionally to keep sauce from sticking.

Cook the pasta until it is about three-quarters done. Drain. Toss with the sauce. Let sit on a warm range, stirring now and then until all excess liquid from the tomatoes is absorbed and the pasta is tender.

Serve with grated pecorino or locatelli cheese.

28
Penne with Tomatoes, Green Olives, and Ricotta Salata
Penne San Vito

There is a glimpse of the Spanish in this intensely flavorful, sweet, and spicy sauce that combines fresh and sun-dried tomatoes. If possible, use fresh hot peppers, as hot as you can take.
You can find ricotta salata at an Italian grocery. It is a crumbly, salty cheese, like feta, but drier. If you can't find it, substitute feta, not fresh ricotta.

1 teaspoon crushed red pepper
1 clove garlic, minced or pressed
½ cup (125 ml) olive oil
2 cups (375 g) chopped onions
¾ lb (375 g) tomatoes, peeled and chopped
¼ lb (125 g) oil-cured sun-dried tomatoes, cut into penne-sized slices
½ lb (250 g) arugula, chopped
8 large oil-cured green olives, pitted and coarsely chopped
1 lb (500 g) penne
½ lb (250 g) ricotta salata cheese, thinly shaved, crumbled, or grated

Heat the red pepper and the garlic in the olive oil. Add the chopped onion and cook over medium-high heat, stirring constantly about five minutes so that the onions will not stick or burn.

Raise to high heat. Add the fresh tomatoes. Sauté one minute, then add the sun-dried tomatoes. Sauté another minute. Now add the arugula and sauté one more minute. Mix in the chopped olives. Lower the heat, cover, and let simmer five minutes. Turn off the heat and keep warm while the penne cooks.

When the penne is just underdone, drain, return to the pot, and toss with the sauce over a warm stove. Let it sit a few minutes.

Serve in bowls with a tablespoon or two of the crumbled ricotta salata cheese on top.

29
Spaghetti with Sun-dried Tomatoes
Spaghetti Putanesca

This is another one of those pastas that is made in almost every region of Italy. *Spaghetti putanesca* means "whore's spaghetti," the implication being that a person spending afternoons screwing around would have no time to shop for a proper dinner and would have to rely on ingredients already in the cupboard, those with long shelf lives and which can be found in almost every Italian kitchen. The essence of *putanesca* is "making do," combining whatever is on hand, from almonds to zucchini, without fuss and without following a recipe.

When making this dish for our friends, we get a little fancy and substitute sun-dried tomatoes (which, if refrigerated, keep indefinitely) for the more ordinary canned ones. It makes a marked refinement in the dish. A few leaves of parsley and basil, freshly picked from the plants in the window box, provide a needed touch of green.

> 2 cloves garlic, pressed or finely chopped
> ½ teaspoon crushed red pepper
> ½ cup (125 ml) olive oil
> ¼ lb (125 g) oil-cured sun-dried tomatoes, coarsely chopped, or one 14-oz (440-g) can Italian plum tomatoes, drained
> 8 oil-cured black olives, pitted and coarsely chopped
> 6 anchovies, rolled with capers
> 12 basil leaves
> 2 tablespoons Italian parsley
> 1 lb (500 g) spaghetti
> grated Parmesan cheese, for the table

Heat the garlic and the pepper in the oil over medium-high heat. Add the tomatoes, olives, and anchovies with capers. Stir briefly. Add the parsley and basil. Cover and turn off the heat.

Keep warm on the stove while the pasta cooks. Before draining, save a few tablespoons of water to add, if necessary, when you toss the pasta with the sauce. Serve with grated Parmesan cheese.

30
Fusilli with Tomato Salsa
Fusilli Estati

This pasta is perfect for a light summer lunch, as an accompaniment to one, or as a first course. It can be served warm as a main course or at room temperature as a salad.

This dish must be made with fresh basil and tomatoes. The sauce is not cooked on the stove, but the ingredients are put in a bowl to "cook" at room temperature. The sauce is then tossed with the cooked pasta.

3 lb (1.5 kg) tomatoes, peeled and coarsely chopped
50 large basil leaves, chopped
¼ cup (30 g) Italian parsley, finely chopped
3 cloves garlic, mashed or pressed
2 tablespoons coarse salt
½ teaspoon crushed red pepper or fresh hot chile pepper
¾ cup (185 ml) olive oil
1 lb (500 g) fusilli

Place the peeled, chopped tomatoes in a bowl. Add the basil, parsley, garlic, salt, pepper, and oil to the tomatoes and mix well. Cover and let stand at room temperature at least one hour. Mix occasionally. The salt will draw the juice from the tomatoes and make a nice oily tomato salsa.

Undercook and drain the pasta. Toss with sauce. There will be quite a bit of liquid which should be completely absorbed before serving.

Variation: Add ½ cup (60 g) shredded mozzarella cheese to the salsa just before you toss it with the fusilli. The warm pasta will melt the cheese slightly.

Artichokes
Carciofi

Artichokes are large, thistlelike perennial plants, native to the Mediterranean region, but extensively cultivated today throughout Europe and in California. To look at and handle an artichoke is to wonder how anyone ever thought to put it in their mouth, let alone consider it a cuisine delicacy. The edible part of the artichoke is the heart and the soft, fleshy bottom part of the leaves after they have been cooked.

To the uninitiated, this prickly vegetable with a heart like fiberglass can present an impenetrable facade. We'll never forget the time cousin Victor brought his uptown girlfriend to Easter dinner. Upon being served a steamed artichoke, a vegetable new to her, she gained entry using a steak knife, put a cross-section of the thistlelike plant in her mouth, and proceeded to chew the leaves and central fuzz, called the choke, with feigned nonchalance. Only when she looked around the table in discomfort and saw the rest of us peeling the leaves, one at a time, and delicately gnawing on their undersides, did she realize her mistake and run gagging from the table.

When using artichokes in recipes, use only the heart and the soft flesh where the stem becomes the vegetable. Discard the fuzzy choke.

To get the heart out of an artichoke: Slice off the stalk and the spiky top. Snap back the outer leaves until you come to leaves that are pale green and tender. Cut large artichokes lengthwise into six or eight sections, small ones into four sections. Cut away the choke and any tough leaves. Rub the sections with a wedge of a lemon and place them in water with lemon juice and a lemon wedge or two to prevent discoloration.

To steam, place on steamer rack over boiling water about five minutes for small artichoke sections and ten minutes for larger pieces. Remove any additional tough leaves at this point.

Fresh baby artichokes are often available. They are extremely tender and do not have a fuzzy choke. If you use them, simply trim a bit of the stem and top, remove any discolored or ragged outer leaves, and steam in acidulated water (lemon juice and water) five to seven minutes. Baby artichokes should be no longer than 2 inches (5 cm). About 10 to 12 of them will make 1 pound (500 g).

If this sounds like a lot of trouble, it is! Artichoke sizes vary, but you'd have to steam somewhere between four and twelve fresh artichokes to get the equivalent of one 14-oz (440-g) can, (8 oz 250

(Continued)

g, drained) or a 9-oz (280-g) package of frozen ones. All these recipes can be made satisfactorily with any of these choices. We prefer frozen to canned. If using canned, avoid artichoke salad or artichokes in strong vinegar solutions.

31
Fettuccine with Artichoke Pesto
Fettuccine con Pesto di Carciofi

How sweet it is! This dish is the easiest to swallow.

6 large (or 8 small) artichoke hearts, sectioned and steamed (see page 65)
  <u>or</u> 2 lb (1 kg) baby artichokes steamed (see page 65)
  <u>or</u> 9 oz (280 g) frozen artichoke hearts, thawed and steamed five minutes
  <u>or</u> 14 oz (440 g) canned artichoke hearts packed in water or oil (no vinegar), drained
2 oz (60 g) salted roasted cashews
2 sprigs parsley
1 clove garlic
2 tablespoons grated Parmesan cheese
squirt of lemon juice
dash of cayenne pepper
¾ cup (185 ml) olive oil
1 lb (500 g) fettucine
¼ lb (125 g) prosciutto, thickly sliced then diced ¼ inch (5 mm)
grated Parmesan cheese, for the table

In a blender or food processor, place the prepared artichokes, cashews, parsley, garlic, cheese, lemon juice, and cayenne pepper. Turn on and add the olive oil slowly, a bit at a time, until the blender blades spin freely, creating a hollow in the center. Add more oil if necessary. Transfer the pesto to a bowl and keep warm on the stove.

Meanwhile, cook the fettucine until nearly *al dente*. Drain, reserving ½ cup (125 ml) of the pasta water on the side. Return the pasta to the pot and sprinkle in the diced prosciutto.

Spoon in the pesto, adding a tablespoon or two of the reserved pasta water as necessary to assure that the sauce coats the pasta evenly. Stir over low heat. Make sure it doesn't stick to the pot; use all the reserved water if necessary. When the ingredients are well mixed and the fettuccine coated with the pesto, the dish is ready.

Serve with freshly grated Parmesan cheese.

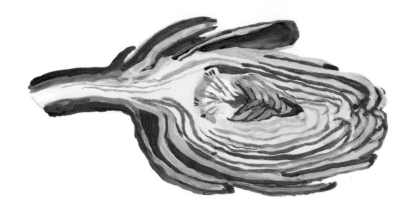

32
Baked Ziti with Artichokes
Ziti al Forno con Carciofi

Because artichokes contain cynarin, a fanciful chemical that stimulates
the sweet receptors in the taste buds, making everything else taste
sweeter than it is, they have been considered the kiss of death to wine.
Thus they have never sat high on the menus of those who dish out fine
cuisine. Maybe we shouldn't, but we like this recipe because of, rather
than in spite of, its baffling flavors. More baked ziti, Ma!

1 large clove garlic, crushed or finely minced

½ teaspoon crushed red pepper

½ cup (125 ml) olive oil

4 to 6 artichokes, cleaned and trimmed (see page 65)

  <u>or</u> 1 lb (500 g) baby artichokes, cleaned and trimmed (see
    page 65)

  <u>or</u> 9 oz (280 g) frozen artichoke hearts, thawed and
    quartered

  <u>or</u> 14 oz (440 g) canned artichoke hearts, drained and
    quartered

½ cup (125 ml) white wine

1 lb (500 g) ziti

1 cup (120 g) Italian parsley, loosely packed

¼ lb (125 g) provolone, grated or cut into small pieces

Preheat the oven to 375° F (190° C/gas 5).

Heat the garlic and crushed pepper in the olive oil. Add the artichokes
and sauté five minutes. Add the wine, cover, and cook over low heat ten
minutes until the artichokes are soft.

Undercook the pasta. Ziti should be firm and somewhat starchy.

Using the empty pasta pot or a large mixing bowl, toss the ziti with
the artichoke mixture, parsley, and provolone. Turn into an oiled baking
dish. Cover and bake twenty minutes.

33
Rigatoni with Artichokes, Bacon, and Eggs
Carbonara Alla Palermitana

This is a Sicilian-style *carbonara*. Any leftovers make a fine
breakfast pasta.

½ cup (125 ml) olive oil

¼ lb (125 g) pancetta, thickly sliced then diced ¼ inch (5
mm)

½ cup (90 g) onion, minced

4 to 6 large artichokes, cleaned and cut into wedges (see
page 65)

   or 1 lb (500 g) baby artichokes, cleaned and trimmed (see
page 65)

   or 9 oz (280 g) frozen artichoke hearts, thawed and
quartered

   or 14 oz (440 g) canned artichokes, drained and
quartered

1 lb (500 g) rigatoni

2 eggs

2 tablespoons (30 g) grated locatelli or Parmesan cheese

¼ cup (30 g) Italian parsley, finely chopped

black pepper, to taste

cayenne pepper, to taste

Add a teaspoon of olive oil to your saucepan and cook the pancetta over medium heat, stirring constantly until you have crispy bacon bits. Remove with a slotted spoon and set aside. Pour off the remaining fat.

Add the remaining olive oil to the pan and sauté onion over medium heat three minutes, until transparent. Then add the artichokes and sauté five minutes. Lower the heat, add ¼ cup (60 ml) of water, cover, and simmer ten or fifteen minutes for canned or frozen artichokes, twenty-five to thirty minutes for fresh ones, stirring now and then, until the artichoke sections are soft. Add the pancetta and cook a few minutes longer.

Begin to cook the rigatoni.

Beat the eggs in a bowl with the cheese, parsley, and black and cayenne peppers.

Drain the pasta when done and transfer it into the saucepan with the artichokes and the pancetta. Pour in the egg mixture and stir over low heat about one minute until the cheese and eggs form a coating around the pasta. Serve.

34
Spaghettini with Artichokes
Pasta con Carciofini

Often, in the spring, baby artichokes, 2 inches (5 cm) long from tip to stem, are available in the market. As we said on page 65, if they are small and tender enough, they can be used whole with only the stem and outer layer of leaves removed. (The small chokes are edible.) Trim ½ inch (1 cm) from the stem and the top of the artichoke. Remove the tough outer leaves and steam in water with lemon juice ten minutes. Cut them in half. In cutting, if you notice any tough leaves, remove and discard.
If you can't find baby artichokes, use frozen ones or canned hearts. They are about the same size as baby artichokes.

> ⅔ cup (170 ml) olive oil
>
> 3 cloves garlic thinly sliced
>
> 1 teaspoon crushed red pepper
>
> 1 lb (500 g) baby artichokes, cleaned, trimmed, and cut in half (see page 65)
>
> > <u>or</u> 9 oz (280 g) frozen artichoke hearts, thawed and quartered
> >
> > <u>or</u> 14 oz (440 g) canned artichoke hearts, drained and quartered
>
> ½ lb (250 g) tomatoes, peeled and chopped
>
> 2 tablespoons Italian parsley, finely chopped
>
> 1 teaspoon salt-cured capers
>
> 1 lb (500 g) spaghettini
>
> grated Parmesan cheese, for the table

Place the olive oil in your saucepan, add the garlic and pepper and sauté a minute or two until the garlic starts to turn brown. Add the artichokes and sauté five minutes. Add the tomatoes, parsley, and capers. Lower the heat and cook covered ten minutes. The artichokes should be tender, and there should be a good amount of liquid.

Cook the pasta and drain when it is still slightly underdone. Mix well with the artichoke sauce in the pasta pot, and let it sit on a warm range while the pasta absorbs the liquid.

Serve with grated Parmesan cheese.

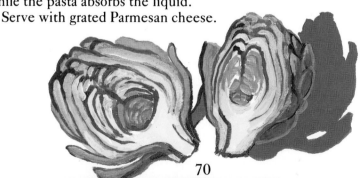

Pumpkin
Zucca

In the autumn, fresh pumpkins are available in the markets. Cooked, they have a mild flavor and soft consistency that we find sweet and nostalgic. If you have never gone further with a pumpkin than carving jack-o'-lanterns, here's what to do with the beast. For sauce, a small pumpkin (2 to 3 lb/1 kg) is best. Use a sharp paring knife to dig out the stem. Then cut the pumpkin lengthwise into quarters. Scrape out the seeds. (These can be dried in the oven or sun, shelled, and eaten separately.) Peel the slices with an ordinary potato peeler, then slice and dice as called for in the recipe.

35
Ravioli with Pumpkin Sauce
Ravioli con Sugo di Zucca

In recent years, many restaurants have begun to offer ravioli stuffed with pumpkin. Here is a variation that has the pumpkin on the outside. If you choose to use the pumpkin seeds as a garnish, and you do not wish to go through the trouble of drying and shelling them yourself, you may buy them already shelled.

Again, notice that this recipe calls for 2 pounds (1 kg) of ravioli, and it will serve four to six.

½ cup (125 ml) olive oil

2 oz (60 g) prosciutto, thickly sliced then diced ¼ inch (5 mm)

½ teaspoon crushed red pepper

2 to 3 lb (1 kg) pumpkin, peeled and diced ½ inch (1 cm)

2 tablespoons Italian parsley, finely chopped

12 large basil leaves

¾ teaspoon ground nutmeg

¼ teaspoon thyme

2 lb (1 kg) cheese ravioli (we prefer the smaller ravioli, 36 to 48 count to the pound/500 g)

¼ cup (60 g) shelled pepitas (pumpkin seeds), roasted, (optional)

grated Parmesan cheese, for the table

Put 1 tablespoon (15 ml) of the olive oil in a saucepan and brown the prosciutto over medium heat, about five minutes. Add the remaining oil, the pepper, and the pumpkin. Raise the heat and sauté another five minutes, stirring constantly, until the pumpkin starts to soften. Add the parsley, basil, nutmeg, and thyme. Lower heat, cover, and simmer twenty minutes until the pumpkin has melted down and is very soft.

Cook the ravioli *al dente* and drain. Toss with the pumpkin sauce. Garnish individual portions with roasted pepitas, if you wish. Serve with grated Parmesan cheese.

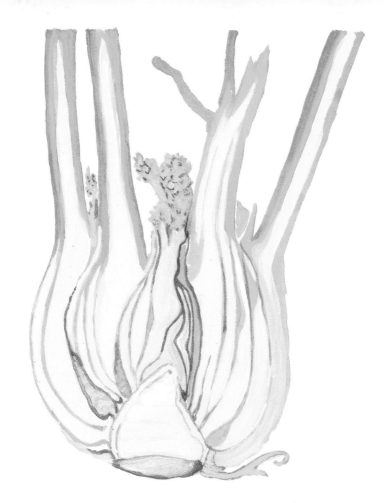

Fennel
Finocchio

Fennel, a member of the parsley family, grows wild around the Mediterranean region. In recent years, it has become very popular and is now cultivated and widely available. In Italy, fennel has long been used as a flavoring herb or vegetable, and it is eaten as an appetizer or in-between-course digestive at large feasts.

When choosing fennel, select firm, tightly packed bulbs. The feathery top part should be green and the bulb should be white.

To prepare: Cut away the feathery top to where the bulb starts to swell. Remove the tough, stringy outer stalks until you reach the firm, crisp part of the bulb. This is the "heart." Trim the base to remove any woody parts, and proceed according to the recipe's instructions.

Raw fennel has the taste of anise or mild licorice. Cooked fennel is mildly flavored.

36
Linguine with Fennel Pesto
Linguine con Finocchio

The following dish, a fennel pesto, makes a good appetizer before a heavy meat-and-potatoes second course or a wonderful light main course.

½ cup (125 ml) olive oil
2 bulbs fennel (approximately 2 lb/1 kg before cleaning), cleaned (see page 73) and chopped into small pieces
1 lb (500 g) tomatoes, peeled and chopped into small pieces
10 basil leaves
½ teaspoon dried oregano
½ teaspoon crushed red pepper
1 lb (500 g) linguine

Place ¼ cup (60 ml) of oil in the saucepan and sauté the fennel between five to ten minutes over medium heat, stirring constantly. When the fennel starts to soften and become transparent, add the tomatoes and stir briefly. Remove from heat and let cool. Put the mixture in a blender or food processor with the basil and oregano. Purée. Set aside.

Put the remaining ¼ cup (60 ml) of oil along with the pepper flakes into the saucepan. Heat on high until the pepper begins to pop. Just before the oil starts to smoke, add the purée. Quick-fry, stirring constantly, over high heat thirty seconds or so. Lower the heat, cover, and simmer fifteen minutes.

Cook the linguine until almost *al dente*. Toss with the fennel-tomato pesto over a warm stove, seeing that all the liquid is absorbed and the pasta and the sauce are thoroughly mixed.

37
Angel Hair with Fennel Sauce
Capellini al Gabriello

Here is another Sicilian sauce in which you taste the influence of North African cooking with its curious mix of sweet and savory flavors. This dish has heaven's scent. Legend has it that Sant'Agata di Militello, a Sicilian mystic of the tenth century, was especially devoted to the Archangel Gabriel and that she created this dish in honor of her visions and audiences with that divine messenger.

> 1 tablespoon currants
> pinch saffron
> ½ cup (125 ml) of white wine
> ½ cup (90 g) of blanched, slivered almonds
> 2 tablespoons pine nuts
> ½ cup (125 ml) olive oil
> ½ teaspoon crushed red pepper
> 1 cup (185 g) onion, finely chopped
> 2 bulbs fennel (1½ to 2 lb/1 kg), trimmed (see page 73) and
>   chopped to yield approximately 3 cups (500 g)
> 1 lb (500 g) capellini

Soak the currants and the saffron in the wine thirty minutes. Toast the almonds and pine nuts in a heavy pan, remove, and set aside. For tips on light pan roasting, see recipe (54).

Heat the olive oil with the red pepper in a large pan or wok, add the onion, and sauté over high heat two minutes. Add the fennel and continue cooking over high heat, stirring constantly, another two minutes.

Add the currant, wine, and saffron mixture to the pan. Stir vigorously one minute, then add the toasted almonds and pine nuts. Lower the heat to a slow simmer, cover, and cook slowly twenty-five to thirty minutes, stirring occasionally.

When the fennel sauce is almost done, cook the capellini. Drain and toss with the sauce.

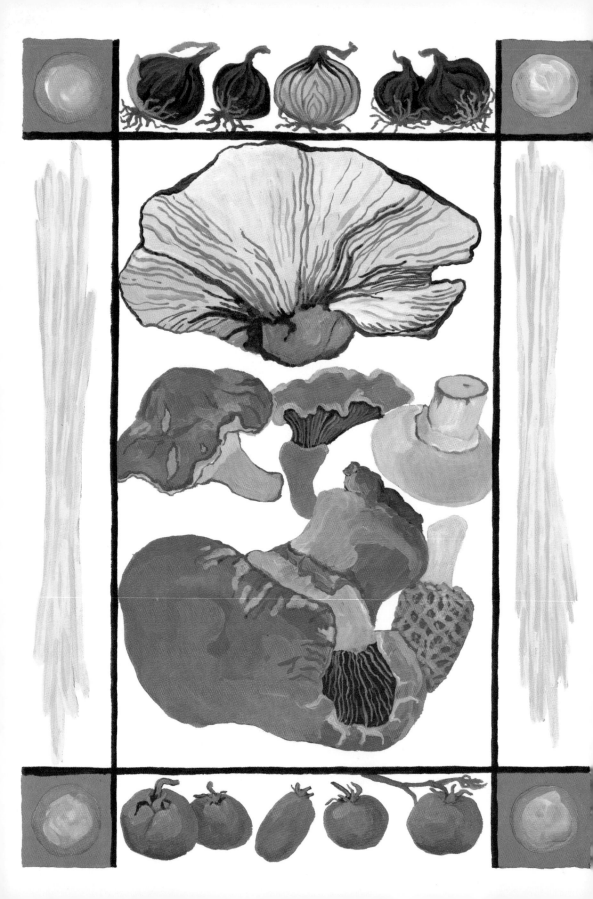

Mushrooms
Fungi

Although large areas of Sicily are dry and therefore not the best environment for mushrooms—which need damp, dark places to flourish—those who know where to look can find many varieties of edible mushrooms. Porcini and other dried mushrooms have been imported for some time and are enjoyed in a great many ways. Lately, the presence of exotic fungi in the markets has, indeed, mushroomed. And so we find uses for giant portabellos, shiitakes, oyster mushrooms, chanterelles, morels, and other children of the night. Mushrooms have a moony character and can imbue a dish with their lush, primal flavor.

38
Spaghettini with Mushrooms
Sugo di Fungi Rosso

Here is a recipe for a red mushroom sauce. Ordinary packaged mushrooms can be used, but you might try the more exotic varieties. Mushrooms have a tendency to "melt," so use only meaty types. For this dish, we recommend portabello mushrooms.

1 cup (185 g) onion, minced
1 clove garlic, crushed or finely minced
½ teaspoon crushed red pepper
½ cup (125 ml) olive oil
1½ lb (750 g) portabello mushrooms, bottom of stems removed then caps cut into small pieces (if using ordinary mushrooms, cut lengthwise in thirds)
¼ cup (30 g) Italian parsley, finely chopped
1 lb (500 g) tomatoes, peeled and chopped into small pieces
3 oz (90 g) tomato paste
1 lb (500 g) spaghettini
grated Parmesan cheese, for the table

Sauté the onion, garlic, and pepper in the olive oil over medium heat five minutes, stirring constantly. Raise heat, add the mushrooms, and sauté three to five minutes until mushrooms are reduced in size and have given up their moisture. Add the parsley and tomatoes. Stir over high heat two minutes longer. Lower the heat and add the tomato paste, mixing well. Cover and simmer slowly fifteen minutes.

Cook the spaghettini, drain, and toss with the mushroom sauce. Serve with grated Parmesan cheese.

39
Fettuccine with Wild Mushrooms
Fettucine al Fungi di Bosco

Every time we tried to cook a mushroom dish that would do justice to our stony Uncle Tonno's memories of mushroom gathering in the Sicilian woods of his childhood, we met with his silent disappointment. We used ordinary supermarket mushrooms. But we never gave up our goal of finding a fungus that would transport Tonno to his native countryside. Success finally arrived in the early '80s along with the invasion of the luxury mushrooms. Uncle Tonno was so happy he nearly smiled.

¾ lb (375 g) shiitake mushrooms
¾ lb (375 g) portabello mushrooms
½ cup (125 ml) olive oil
2 tablespoons (30 g) butter
¼ cup (30 g) Italian parsley, finely chopped
¼ teaspoon ground black pepper
1 lb (500 g) fettuccine

Clean the mushrooms well, remove tough stems, and slice the caps and remaining stems into strips ¼ inch (5 mm) wide.

Put the olive oil and butter in a heavy skillet. When the oil heats and the butter starts to sizzle, toss the mushrooms into the pan, stirring constantly over medium-high heat three minutes. Add the parsley, stir to mix, lower the heat, cover the pan, and cook another four to five minutes, stirring occasionally. During this time, the mushrooms will give off their tasty liquid.

Remove the mushrooms from the heat. Add the black pepper.

Cook the fettuccine, drain, and toss with the sauce. Serve immediately.

Note: You may substitute 3 oz (90 g) dried porcini mushrooms for the shiitake-portabello combination. Just cover them in water and soak at least twenty minutes, or until they are plumped. Save 2 tablespoons of the liquid to add to the sauce for the last four to five minutes of cooking, and pour the rest of the liquid into the pasta water for flavor.

40
Spaghetti with Mushroom Pesto
Pasta con Pesto Porcini

With all the novel and *nouvelle* mushrooms we find in today's markets we have never come upon fresh porcinis; therefore, we always use the dried article. We usually soak and reconstitute them in tomatoes, wine, or some other liquid ingredient we will later use in
the recipe.
We adapted this northern Italian recipe from the late Pauly "the Mushroom" Titone, the fungus among us, our good friend who manned the kitchen over at Randazzo's Pizza for almost thirty years and who had an amazing variety of mushroom recipes.

> 2 oz (60 g) dried porcini mushrooms
> ¾ lb (375 g) tomatoes, peeled, and chopped very small
> ½ cup (125 ml) olive oil
> ½ cup (90 g) chopped shallots (spring onions)
> 1 clove garlic, peeled
> ¼ cup (60 g) pine nuts
> 4 anchovies, rinsed and drained
> 1 tablespoon rosemary
> 2 tablespoons Italian parsley
> 1 tablespoon (15 g) sweet butter
> ¾ teaspoon crushed red pepper
> 1 lb (500 g) spaghetti

Rinse the mushrooms to remove any sand or grit. Put them in a bowl with the chopped tomatoes and let them sit thirty minutes.

Place ¼ cup (60 ml) of the olive oil in a food processor or blender. Add the mushrooms, tomatoes, shallots, garlic, pine nuts, anchovies, rosemary, and parsley. Chop until you have a chunky pesto purée.

Melt the butter and heat the remaining ¼ cup (60 ml) of olive oil and the crushed red pepper in your sauce pot. Add the pesto and stir over medium heat one minute. Lower the heat, cover, and simmer fifteen minutes, stirring frequently to keep the sauce from sticking.

Cook the pasta and toss with the sauce.

Peppers
Peperoni

There are more ways than one to skin a sweet pepper. The neatest way is to put the peppers on aluminum foil under a hot broiler (griller), gas or electric, turning as needed to make sure the skin bubbles, blackens, and separates evenly. They are then ready to peel. Remove them from the oven and run under cold water to stop from cooking further. Split them open and discard the seeds and the stem base. Peel off the blackened skin. And there you have it.

If you have a gas range you can toss the peppers directly onto the burner, turning them over to see that they blacken evenly. Then skin them as above.

41
Rigatoni with Roast Peppers
Rigatoni ai Peperoni Tricolori

This dish is colorful and simply delicious. It is perfectly tasty at room temperature, and without the cheese, it can be served as a party food, a roast pepper–pasta salad.

> ¾ teaspoon crushed red pepper or fresh chili to taste
> ⅓ cup (85 ml) olive oil
> 6 to 8 assorted sweet peppers (3 lb/1½ kg) yellow, red, and green, roasted, and cut into rigatoni-sized strips
> 1 lb (500 g) rigatoni
> grated Parmesan cheese, for the table

Heat the hot pepper in the olive oil in a sauce pot. Add the roasted sweet peppers, stir a minute or so over high heat, reduce the heat, cover, and let simmer slowly fifteen minutes.

Cook rigatoni until tender. Toss with the peppers.

Serve with grated Parmesan cheese.

Beans
Fagioli

The cultivation of the bean goes hand-in-hand with the development of agriculture. Beans could be dried and stored, then used as a source of energy during the lean months. The Egyptian pictogram for the bean is a sun inside a body, and inside the tombs of the pharaohs, golden beans were discovered, symbolic subsistence for soul's journey through the Night. Excellent sources of protein and fiber, building blocks for strong bodies and positive spirits, beans and legumes have maintained their reputation as "a mystical fruit" into modern times. As ancient a food as grain, they go well with pasta. There are endless variations of *pasta e fagioli,* a dish that has been with us since Roman times.

Fresh beans are ideal and should be used whenever possible. With interest in "green" eating on the rise, more varieties are becoming available in the markets. Since winters are short and mild in Sicily, fresh beans are the order of the day.

Generally, dried beans, the hard-core varieties such as chickpeas and pinto and cannellini beans, must be rinsed in cold water, soaked overnight (four parts water to one part beans), then boiled an hour or so until they are tender yet maintain their shape. If you want to shorten the soaking time to two or three hours instead of overnight, here is a method: Wash the beans and drop them into boiling water. Boil one minute. This will break the skin and hasten absorption. Turn off the heat and let them sit two and a half hours, and they will be ready to cook.

Lentils and softer beans, such as dried fava and lima beans, use less water and need only about an hour of soaking time. They cook more quickly, too. If you have extra time to cook them, you can dispense with soaking.

Never put salt in the water until after the beans are cooked. It interferes with the beans' absorption of water.

Canned beans are easier to use and require no forethought except to have them on hand.

Of course, if you soak and cook the beans yourself, you want to add any bean water left over after the beans are cooked to the pasta pot, using it to flavor the water in which the pasta is boiled. Even if you use canned beans, we suggest you drain them in a strainer over the pasta pot. Since, normally, beans will be packed in brine, you will be adding some salt to the water. Check the water for saltiness and reduce the amount of additional salt accordingly.

42
Spaghetti with Lima Beans

This first recipe is quick because lima beans do not require precooking.

1 tablespoon (15 g) butter
¼ cup (60 ml) olive oil
½ cup (185 g) purple onion, chopped
⅓ teaspoon crushed red pepper
1 clove garlic, crushed or minced
¾ lb (375 g) tomato, peeled, cut into chunks
12 large basil leaves
1½ cups (280 g) baby lima beans (fresh, or, if frozen, thawed)
1 lb (500 g) spaghetti
grated Parmesan cheese, for the table

Melt the butter in the oil. Add the onion, pepper, and garlic and sauté over medium-high heat until onion is soft, about five minutes. Add the tomatoes, basil, and beans. Stir one minute. Lower the heat. Cover and simmer five minutes, or until beans are tender. (If you use frozen beans and do not defrost them, they will take five or ten minutes longer.)

Toss with cooked pasta. Serve with grated Parmesan cheese.

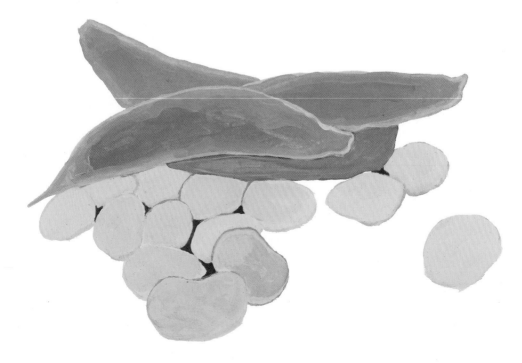

Fava Beans (Broad Beans)
Fave

Fresh fava beans are usually available in vegetable markets only during the spring. As with other legumes, they are best at the beginning of the season. When they are still young, sweet, and tender, they can be eaten raw. The older, larger beans can be bitter and thick skinned. These, however, become quite agreeable after being cooked. Fava beans are something like lima beans, and we have substituted limas in place of them with very satisfying results.

Dried or in cans, fava beans are available all year. The dried beans, if they have their brown outer skins, should be soaked two hours before you cook them. Rinse 1 cup (250 g) of dried beans and soak in 3 cups (750 ml) of water. (If you want to cut the soaking time in half, drop beans into boiling water, turn off the heat, cover, and let sit one hour.) Once the beans are rehydrated, remove the thin outer skin. Most often, even well-cooked dried fava beans have skins too tough to eat. Once the skin is removed, the beans will cook firm and tender in fifteen minutes.

As adults, we have come to appreciate the subtle meaty goodness of fava beans, but our earliest experience with them left us feeling deprived and outcast. With a pack of cousins, we were herded off by Grandma Adela to see Cecil B. DeMille's epic film *The Ten Commandments*. She packed us snacks: salami sandwiches and several pounds of fresh fava beans. She passed the latter around as hors d'oeuvres even before Moses had been found in the bulrushes. During the three-hour spectacle, the empty bean pods accumulated at our feet, while our taste buds yearned for the mysteries of the popcorn and Raisinets which we heard being crunched in the dark all around us.

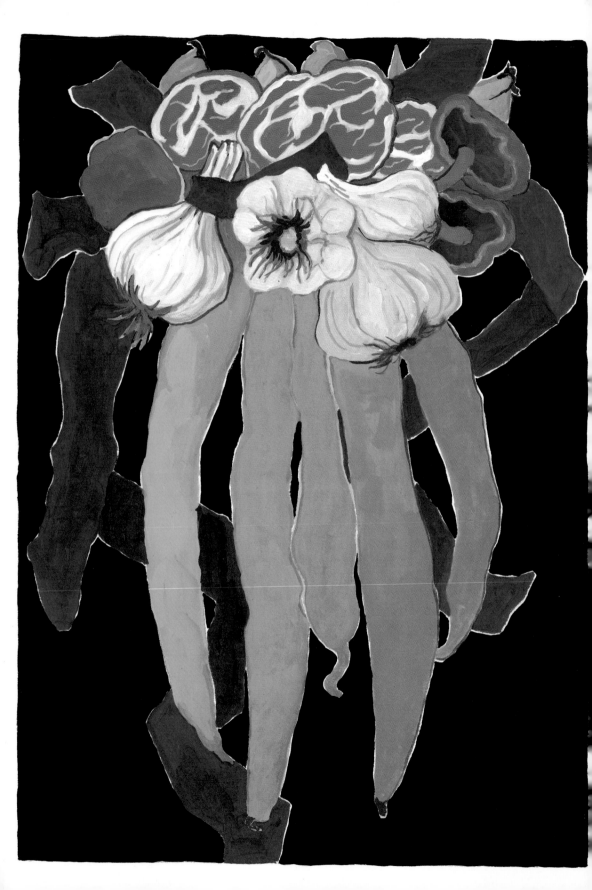

43

Linguine with Fava Beans, Porcini Mushrooms, and Pancetta

Linguine al Fave con Porcini e Pancetta

In addition to fava beans, this recipe features Italian bacon and porcini mushrooms, both available in Italian markets. Porcini mushrooms have a meatier scent, taste, and texture than the pork. The beans have a strong flavor, too. This is a hearty dish, perfect for a cool spring night. If using dried fava beans, they need not be precooked, simply well soaked, with the skins removed.

> 1 lb (500 g) tomatoes, peeled and cut into small pieces
> 1½ oz (45 g) dried porcini mushrooms, broken into small bits
> ¼ lb (125 g) pancetta thickly sliced then diced ¼ inch (5 mm)
> ⅓ cup (85 ml) olive oil
> 1 clove garlic, crushed or finely minced
> ¼ teaspoon crushed red pepper
> 2 tablespoons Italian parsley, finely minced
> 1½ cups shelled fava beans
>   or ¾ cup dried fava beans, soaked two hours and skinned
> 1 lb (500 g) linguine
> grated Parmesan cheese, for the table

In a mixing bowl, combine the peeled tomatoes with the dried mushroom bits, mixing frequently to make sure all the mushrooms absorb the juice from the tomatoes.

Cut the bacon into small pieces. Heat 1 teaspoon (15 ml) of the olive oil in your saucepot, add the pancetta, and fry over medium heat. Scramble it around constantly until the bacon bits become crisp and golden brown on all sides.

Remove the pancetta with a slotted spoon. Drain off any accumulated fat. Add the cooked pancetta to the bowl with the porcinis and tomatoes.

Heat the remaining olive oil, garlic, and red pepper over high heat. When the garlic begins to brown, add the tomato-pancetta-porcini mixture. Stir one minute over medium-high heat. Add the parsley and fava beans and simmer, about ten to twenty minutes, until beans are tender.

Cook pasta *al dente*. Toss with other ingredients. Let sit until all liquid from the tomatoes is absorbed.

Serve with grated Parmesan cheese.

44
Spaghetti with Fresh Fava Bean Pesto
Spaghetti al Fave

This recipe can be made with dried fava beans. The taste will be satisfying, but the color will not. Canned cannellini beans will do nicely, but again, the color will be grayish. Fresh lima beans are the closest alternative, although a bit more starchy than the fava beans.

> 1½ cup (280 g) fava beans (1½ to 2 lb/1 kg, in the pod)
> 1 cup (185 g) minced onion
> ⅔ cup (170 ml) olive oil
> 1 lb (500 g) tomatoes, peeled and chopped into small pieces
> ¼ cup (30 g) Italian parsley, finely chopped
> 1 teaspoon oregano
> ½ teaspoon crushed red pepper
> 1 lb (500 g) spaghetti
> grated Parmesan cheese, for the table

Boil the fava beans ten minutes in water to cover. Meanwhile, sauté the onion in ¼ cup (60 ml) of the oil over medium heat. Place the onion, cooked beans, tomatoes, parsley, and oregano in a blender or food mill. Purée. If the mixture seems stiff, add a tablespoon or so of the water in which you cooked the beans.

Heat the pepper in the remaining ¼ cup (60 ml) of olive oil over high heat. Add the bean purée. Reduce the heat and simmer on low fifteen minutes, stirring occasionally to prevent sticking.

Cook the pasta, drain, and toss with the pesto (the purée). Serve with grated Parmesan cheese.

Chickpeas
Ceci

Dried chickpeas, also known as garbanzos, must be soaked overnight, then boiled an hour or so, four parts water to one part beans. However, canned chickpeas are much easier to use, and we've never seen fresh ones available.

45
Perciatelli with Chickpeas and Hot Peppers
Ceci e Peppy

Here's a recipe you can make quickly from items in your cupboard.
The chickpeas complete the pepper like thunder completes lightning.
This dish not only lights you up, but is a boom to a sluggish digestion.
A word of warning: have your fun, but don't get too peppy. The recipe
calls for 1 ½ teaspoons of crushed red pepper: a formidable amount for
four. This may have to be adjusted, but we think that this is the
amount that will make the dish perfectly blistering but still edible.
A word about fresh hot peppers: Just as different people have different
temperaments, fresh peppers are hot to different degrees. The ¼ cup
(30 g) we advise might be too much or too little. Sample a seed of the
pepper beforehand and take your reaction to it into account when
seasoning the sauce. Better safe than sizzling.
Perciatelli, sometimes called bucatini, is a long, thick round pasta with
a thin hole down the center. If you cannot find it, substitute spaghetti.

4 cloves garlic, sliced

¼ cup red or green chile, jalapenos, cherry hots, or a similar
variety, minced (use the seeds!)

or 1½ teaspoons crushed red pepper

½ cup (125 ml) olive oil

¼ cup (30 g) sweet red pepper (miniatures if possible), very
thinly sliced

½ lb (250 g) tomatoes peeled and chopped

1 cup (185 g) cooked chickpeas

1 lb (500 g) perciatelli

Sauté the garlic and hot pepper in the olive oil one minute over medium-high heat, stirring constantly. Add the sliced sweet pepper and continue stirring over medium-high heat two minutes. Raise the heat. Add
the tomatoes and chickpeas. Continue stirring over high heat one minute. Lower the heat, cover, and simmer slowly five minutes.

Undercook the perciatelli. Drain, return to the pot, and toss with the
sauce on a hot burner thirty seconds. Cover, remove from heat, and let
sit until all the liquid is absorbed.

46
Fusilli with Chickpea Pesto
Pesto Ceci Arabiatta

This dish shows the Middle Eastern influence. It has something in common with both baba ghanoush and hummus. The following recipe will coat easily two pounds (1 kg) of pasta. We like to make more than we need; the other half is good later in the week as a dip for chips or on wedges of pita bread.

1 lb (500 g) eggplant (aubergine) whole
1 cup (185 g) cooked chickpeas,
¾ lb (375 g) tomatoes, peeled and chopped
2 tablespoons pine nuts
1 cup (120 g) Italian parsley
¼ cup (60 ml) fresh lemon juice
1 clove garlic, peeled
½ teaspoon crushed red pepper
⅓ cup (85 ml) olive oil
1 lb (500 g) fusilli

Perforate the eggplant with a fork in several places and bake in a pre-heated 400° F (200° C/gas 6) oven forty-five minutes to an hour, or until it is soft and cooked throughout. Let it cool enough to handle, then cut in half, scrape out the pulp, and place in a blender or food processor.

Add the chickpeas, tomatoes, pine nuts, parsley, lemon juice, garlic, and red pepper. Then blend, adding the oil a little at a time until the mixture spins freely. It should be the consistency of thick soup, not watery. If it is too thin, add extra chickpeas, pine nuts, and parsley.

Cook the fusilli extra *al dente*. Drain. Return to the pot and add the pesto, mixing as you add, until you have coated the pasta. Warm over a gentle flame a minute or two until the sauce heats through and the pasta cooks fully. Serve.

Extra pesto will keep several days in the refrigerator.

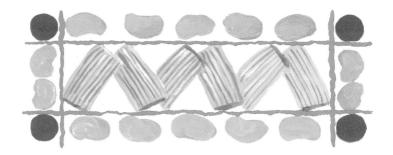

47
Pasta and Cannellini Beans, Sicilian Style
Pasta e Fagioli

In this recipe, fennel, which gives that characteristic sweet Sicilian flavor, is substituted for celery, an ingredient found in most northern Italian pasta-and-bean dishes. A bit of ham is added to provide some body and flavor. Again, as in other recipes in this section, the pasta dominates the beans. To make *pasta e fagioli* soup, add 6 cups (1 ½ liters) of water and use half the amount of pasta, cooked right in with the beans.

This recipe calls for cannellini beans (white kidney beans). Fresh are rare. If you use dried, about three quarters of a cup soaked and cooked will yield what you need for the recipe. Popular import companies offer 19-oz (590-g) can of cannellini beans, which, when drained, is approximately the amount you need for a pound (500 g) of pasta.

> ¾ teaspoon crushed red pepper
> ½ cup (125 ml) olive oil
> 1½ cups (280 g) purple onion, chopped
> 1 cup (185 g) fennel, cleaned and chopped (see page 73)
> ¼ lb (125 g) prosciutto, thickly sliced then diced ¼ inch (5 mm)
> 2 cups (375 g) cooked cannellini beans
> 1 lb (500 g) tomatoes, peeled and diced
> ¼ cup (30 g) Italian parsley, chopped
> 1 teaspoon dried oregano
> 1 lb (500 g) rigatoni
> grated Parmesan or Romano cheese, for the table

Heat the red pepper in the oil over medium-high heat, add the onion and sauté three minutes. Add the fennel and sauté three minutes longer.

Raise the heat, add the prosciutto, and fry until just brown around the edges. Add the beans, then the tomatoes, parsley, and oregano and sauté one minute. Lower heat, cover, and simmer fifteen minutes.

Cook the pasta and toss with the beans. Serve with grated Parmesan or Romano cheese.

Lentils
Lenticchie

The Roman poet Horace once wrote, "Cor populum Romani est ubi esculentae sunt." The heart of the Roman people is where the lentils are. Cheap day labor could be had for a pound of dried lentils. In the ancient Mediterranean world and throughout the Near and Middle East, lentils were as common as dirt, and today they still come cheaply.

Lentils are a simple food no doubt, but that doesn't mean they can't be satisfying. We find ourselves turning to them in the cold months. Here are two dishes, filling and tasty, that combine the lentils with other vegetables and small amounts of meat. We prefer the meat as a flavoring rather than as a prominent ingredient, but do not hesitate to add more meat if you like a heartier dish.

Canned lentils are sometimes available in Middle Eastern or Italian grocery stores. If you can't find them, boil your own. They cook much faster than beans. Wash lentils thoroughly. Soak ½ cup (125 g) lentils one hour in 1½ cups (375 ml) of cold water. Then boil thirty to forty minutes. This will yield approximately 1 cup (185 g) of cooked lentils. If there is any water left, drain it into the pasta water.

48
Orecchiette with Lentils and Escarole
Pasta con Lenticchie

Orecchiette are small, ear-shaped pasta. If you cannot find them, small shells will do. Good quality fennel sausage is available in Italian groceries.

> ¼ lb (125 g) fennel sausage, aproximately one large or two small links
> ½ teaspoon crushed red pepper
> ½ cup (125 ml) olive oil
> 1 lb (500 g) escarole, finely sliced
> 1 cup (185 g) lentils, precooked (see page 90) or canned
> 1 lb (500 g) orecchiette
> grated Parmesan, pecorino, or locatelli cheese, for the table

Remove the sausage casing and discard, leaving just the meat. Heat the red pepper in two tablespoons of the olive oil in the sauce pot. Add the sausage meat and sauté over medium-high heat until it begins to brown, about five minutes.

Raise the heat and add the remaining olive oil. Add the escarole gradually, stirring to reduce. Cook a minute or two, stirring constantly.

Add the lentils. Lower heat, cover, and cook another ten minutes.

Cook orecchiette until almost done. Drain, return to the pot, and toss with the other ingredients over low heat, making sure that they are thoroughly mixed.

Serve with your choice of grated cheese.

Variations: Spinach can be substituted for escarole. The dish will be a bit drier, so you will have to add an additional tablespoon or two of oil or pasta water to make it work.

If you would like to make a nice escarole soup, soak the lentils in 6 cups (1½ liters) of water, but don't precook. After you sauté the escarole, add the lentils and the water and boil slowly thirty-five to forty minutes, or until the lentils are almost soft. Add only ¼ lb (125 g) of orecchiette and cook an additional ten minutes, until the pasta is done.

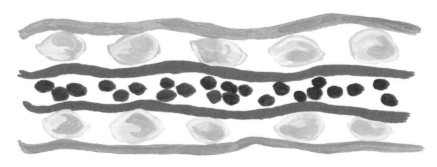

49
Linguine with Lentil Ragusa
Linguine Alla Nina

Here is Uncle Tonno's barber's wife's best friend Nina's recipe for
linguine with a lentil sauce.

¼ lb (125 g) ground lamb
1 tablespoon lemon juice
1 tablespoon (15 g) butter
¼ cup (60 ml) olive oil
1 clove garlic, minced
½ teaspoon crushed red pepper
½ cup (90 g) onion, finely diced
½ cup (90 g) celery, finely diced
1 lb (500 g) tomatoes, peeled and chopped
1 tablespoon tomato paste
½ teaspoon dried oregano
1 tablespoon Italian parsley, finely chopped
¼ teaspoon rosemary
1 cup (185 g) lentils, precooked (see page 90) or canned
1 lb (500 g) linguine
grated Parmesan, pecorino, or locatelli cheese, for the table

Sprinkle the lamb with the lemon juice.

Melt the butter and heat the olive oil in your saucepan. Add the garlic,
red pepper, and onion and sauté three minutes over medium-high heat.
Add the celery and continue sautéing another three to five minutes until
the onion and celery begin to soften.

Add the lamb and brown on all sides, about five minutes. Break up
any clumps as you brown it.

Add tomatoes, tomato paste, oregano, parsley, and rosemary. Stir well.
Now lower the heat, cover, and cook five minutes.

Add the lentils and continue simmering another ten minutes.

Cook the pasta and drain.

This sauce is thick. Toss a few spoonfuls of the sauce with the cooked
pasta to keep it from getting stiff and wiry. The rest of the sauce should
be ladled on top of each serving.

Serve with your choice of grated cheese.

50
Mixed Bean Salad with Bowties
Insalata di Fagioli Misto con Farfalle

This salad can be prepared ahead of time and taken out of the
refrigerator to reach room temperature. As with many pasta dishes, the
flavors becomes more homogenized and pleasing by lolling around
together. In this recipe, we use chickpeas, and lima and kidney beans,
but you may substitute canellini or fava beans, or even fresh peas,
depending on what is available at the market.

¾ cup (155 g) chickpeas, drained
¾ cup (155 g) lima beans, drained
¾ cup (155 g) red kidney beans, drained
1 cup (185 g) purple onion, finely chopped
½ cup (90 g) celery, finely chopped
½ cup (90 g) fennel, finely chopped
¼ cup (30 g) parsley, minced
¼ cup (60 ml) red wine vinegar
1 clove garlic, peeled
1 tablespoon Dijon mustard
salt and pepper, to taste
¾ cup (185 ml) olive oil
1 lb (500 g) farfalle

Put all beans and vegetables in a large bowl. In a blender, blend the
vinegar, garlic, mustard, and salt and pepper at high speed thirty to forty-
five seconds. Remove the cover and slowly pour the olive oil into the
blender in a slow stream until it is well mixed.

If mixing by hand, place the vinegar, garlic, finely minced or pressed,
mustard, and salt and pepper in a bowl. Beat with a fork or whisk until
the ingredients are well mixed. Then slowly pour the olive oil into the
bowl, whisking constantly until all the olive oil is added and it is well
blended.

Add the vinaigrette dressing to the beans and vegetables and mix well.

Cook the farfalle, drain, and mix well with the bean salad. Let stand
at room temperature five or ten minutes and mix again to make sure the
noodles absorb the dressing evenly. Serve immediately or refrigerate. If
refrigerated, remove at least twenty minutes before serving.

Peas
Piselli

Fresh peas are widely available all year round. We find that frozen baby peas are an excellent substitute for the fresh and always like to keep a package in the freezer for use in an unexpected meal. Fresh or frozen, never cook the peas; simply add them at the end of the cooking. The heat of the dish will cook them perfectly. If you do use the frozen, defrost them before adding to the dish.

51
Spaghetti with Peas and Prosciutto
Spaghetti con Piselli

Salty ham and sweet peas.

1 tablespoon (15 g) butter
¼ cup (60 ml) olive oil
1 clove garlic, pressed or finely minced
½ teaspoon crushed red pepper
1 cup (185 g) onion, diced
¼ lb (125 g) prosciutto, thickly sliced then diced ¼ inch (5 mm)
1 lb (500 g) tomatoes, peeled and chopped
1 tablespoon Italian parsley, finely chopped
12 basil leaves
1½ cups (280 g) baby peas (fresh or frozen)
1 lb (500 g) spaghetti
grated Parmesan cheese, for the table

Heat the butter in the olive oil over medium heat. Add the garlic, pepper, and onion. Sauté, stirring constantly, about five minutes until the onion is soft and transparent. Add the diced prosciutto and sauté two minutes more until it begins to brown. Add the tomatoes, parsley, and basil. Lower heat. Cover and cook five minutes. Turn off heat and add the peas, mixing them thoroughly with the hot sauce to warm them through. Peas should be virtually raw.

Cook the pasta. Toss with the other ingredients. Serve with grated Parmesan cheese.

Onions
Cipolla

52
Spaghetti with Onions
Spaghetti con Cipolli

Here we have one of the simplest dishes to make, using just a few cupboard staples. Cooking brings out the onions' complexity. It intensifies their sweetness and brings them to a consistency almost like carmel. Served with grated cheese, this dish is somewhat reminiscent of the French *soupe a l'oignon gratinée*. Ideally, prepare this recipe in a pressure cooker; this will produce a good amount of thick, syrupy sauce from the onions.

> 3 lb (1½ kg) yellow onions, sliced
> ⅔ cup (170 ml) olive oil
> ½ teaspoon crushed red pepper
> 1 lb (500 g) spaghetti
> grated Parmesan cheese, for the table

Sauté the sliced onions in the olive oil with the crushed pepper over high heat ten minutes, stirring constantly. The onions should start to become transparent. Cover tightly, lower the heat, and cook thirty minutes, letting the onions melt down. Stir occasionally to keep them from burning. Some of the onion will become glazed and develop a deep carmel color. If there is not enough liquid, you may add a tablespoon or two of the pasta water during the cooking.

Undercook the spaghetti slightly and mix with the onion sauce, tossing in the pot over a warm range.

Serve with grated Parmesan cheese.

95

Garlic
Aglio

53
Spaghetti with Garlic and Oil
Spaghetti con Aglio Olio

This is one of the most popular of the simple, inexpensive pasta dishes and is the basis of many pasta sauces. Since almost every region in Italy produces its own olive oil, and garlic is grown everywhere, many localities have claimed it as their own invention. Our family swears it was first made in the back-hill village in the Busambra Rock region where our great great grandfather, Luigi Corsi, was born.

1 lb (500 g) spaghetti
6 large garlic cloves, pressed, minced, or sliced
⅓ cup (85 ml) olive oil
½ teaspoon crushed red pepper
  <u>or</u> 1 tablespoon (15 ml) fresh hot chile pepper
¼ cup (30 g) Italian parsley, chopped
2 tablespoons chopped basil (optional)
¼ lb (125 g) fresh tomatoes, peeled and diced (optional)
6 black olives, pitted and chopped (optional)

Bring the pasta water to a boil. Add the spaghetti and start to cook.

While the spaghetti is cooking, heat the oil over medium-high heat and add the garlic and hot pepper. Stir to keep from burning. When the garlic starts to brown, stir in the chopped parsley and remove the sauce from the heat.

If using any optional ingredients, add them at the same time you add the parsley and mix well to heat through.

Drain the pasta and toss with the *aglio olio*.

Variation: Even on the road, our cousin Vinny Penza has to have his pasta and creates sauces he can bottle and keep unrefrigerated for a week. He has been putting his art in jars from Vegas to Valley Stream. Here is his simple and novel way of preparing *aglio olio*.

> **6 garlic cloves, peeled**
> **½ teaspoon crushed red pepper**
> **⅓ cup (85 ml) olive oil**
> **1 lb (500 g) spaghetti**
> **optional ingredients (listed on page 96)**

Preheat the oven to 400°F (200°C/gas 6).

Place the garlic, pepper, oil, and optional ingredients, if you wish, in a large baking dish, cover and bake forty-five minutes. The garlic will brown and become soft. Cook the pasta and toss it right into the steaming hot baking dish. Mix well.

You can also save the sauce for later, down the road.

Nuts
Noci

54
Spaghetti with Fruit and Nuts
Pasta al'Autostrada

Another one of our cousin Vinny's down-home Sicilian-style trail mixes.

2 tablespoons currants
¼ cup (60 ml) white wine
⅓ cup (45 g) toasted pine nuts
½ cup (60 g) walnuts, finely chopped
½ cup (125 ml) olive oil
1 clove garlic, minced
½ teaspoon crushed red pepper
½ cup (90 g) finely chopped shallots (spring onions)
¼ cup (30 g) chopped parsley
1 lb (500 g) spaghetti
grated Parmesan cheese, for the table

Soak currants in wine for half an hour.

Toast the pine nuts by placing them in a heavy pan over high heat. Use no oil or liquid. Keep shaking the pan back and forth over the heat so that the nuts brown evenly and do not burn. This should take about two minutes. When they are done, remove from the pan and set aside with the untoasted walnuts.

Pour the olive oil into the pan, add the garlic, red pepper, and shallots, and sauté over medium heat, stirring often, four to five minutes.

Add the currants with the wine, nuts, and chopped parsley, and continue to cook over medium heat another two to three minutes. Cover, lower the heat, and let simmer ten minutes.

Cook the spaghetti, drain, and toss with the sauce. Serve with grated Parmesan cheese.

Variation. If you care to use anchovies, rinse 4 anchovies and add them to the sauce when you add the nuts. By the time the sauce is done, the anchovies will have cooked down to small bits.

Green Olives
Olivi Verde

55
Green Olive and Parsley Pesto
Pesto Prezzemolo al' olivi Verde

It is important to select fine ingredients for this dish. The parsley
should be fresh, crisp, and deep green and of the sweet Italian variety;
the olives should be oil-cured Sicilian, the large green ones available at
Italian groceries and upscale markets. The garlic and seasoning herbs
in the curing oil gives these olives a lively, yet mellow flavor, and they
are well balanced by the "greenness" of the parsley. The strips of
roasted sweet pepper add an accent, like the pimento in a stuffed olive.

> 1 lb (500 g) oil-cured Sicilian green olives, pitted
>   (1 cup/185 g olive meat)
> 1 cup (120 g) Italian parsley, tightly packed
> ¼ cup (60 g) roasted sweet red pepper (see page 80)
> ½ teaspoon crushed red pepper or fresh red chile pepper
> ¾ cup (185 ml) olive oil
> 1 lb (500 g) spaghetti

Place all the ingredients but the spaghetti in a blender or food processor and homogenize.
Toss with the cooked, drained spaghetti over a warm range.

Pasta with Meats
Carne

On the high protein side of things, our "Uncle" Frank, Aunt Angela's long-time companion, a hard-boiled egg if there ever was one, lives to be over a hundred eating a steady diet of sausages, braciola, salami, and baloney. One of the reasons they never married is that Angela will eat no fat and Frank will eat no lean. He despises salad. He dislikes vegetables unless they are breaded, deep-fried, and served with plenty of cheese.

We heard that in the old days, when they were dating, on rare occasions Aunt Angela would get "Uncle" Frank to come to Sunday dinner. He would only come if she promised that Grandma Adela would make his favorite macaroni dish, meat sauce. Then at the last minute, Aunt Angela would come up with some reason why there was going to be a change in the menu and would take out leftovers from Friday night. She desparately wanted "Uncle" Frank to eat more vegetables, thinking it would calm him down and turn him into more of a domestic sort. But he craved meat, and when he couldn't get it, he'd settle for cheese, and thus always broke Angela's heart by burying her efforts under mountains of Parmesan cheese.

For him, longevity and diet are separate issues. He is adamant about it. "Nobody dies until I say so," he says, "and that includes me."

Sausage
Salsiccia

Buy sausage in an Italian meat store where they take pride in the pork, have a good selection, and guarantee freshness. Fennel and red pepper sausages are the standbys and can be used together, as they are usually the same thickness. However, don't overlook the more unusual sausages, such as those with cheese, lamb, chicken, parsley, or spinach. Different type of sausage can renew a recipe.

Some good pork stores have sausages available already cooked. This will reduce the preparation work. But more often than not, you will have to cook them yourself.

Here are three basic instructions for cooking sausage links.

We like to use a method we call "boil five minutes, broil (grill) five minutes." This works well when the sausage will be cut in rounds and cooked further in the sauce. The combination of boiling (which reduces the fat) and grilling (which brings out the flavor of the meat) is a good one. Place the sausage in a pan, cover with water, prick the sausage, and bring to a rolling boil. Boil five minutes (one to three minutes for thinner sausage). Remove the sausage, pour off the water, and place under a preheated broiler (griller). Turn occasionally to brown evenly, about five minutes.

Place the sausage in a heavy frying pan and cover with water. You may also prick the sausage skin with a fork or knife tip to allow the fatty juices to escape. Turn up the heat and boil uncovered until all the liquid has evaporated. Then lower the heat and pan-fry the sausage in its own fat, turning to brown evenly on all sides.

You may wish to grill the sausage. Put them on the outside barbecue or under the oven broiler (griller), turning them until they are brown on all sides.

In the following recipes, the sausage should be precooked and cut bite-sized into thin slices, either obliquely into ovals or straight across into rounds. Sausage recipe 59 (page 105) has a thick red sauce. The other sausage recipes call for fewer tomatoes. If you want a thicker sauce with any of these, double the amount of tomatoes and add a 6-oz (185-g) can of tomato paste.

56
Ziti with Sausage and Broccoli
Ziti con Salsiccia e Broccoli

This is the meaty version of recipe 11 (page 35).

½ cup (125 ml) olive oil

2 cloves garlic, pressed or minced

½ teaspoon crushed red pepper

2 cups (375 g) broccoli, parboiled and cut into bite-sized
florets (see page 35)

1 lb (500 g) Italian sausage, approximately 4 large links,
cooked and sliced (see preceding page 101)

1 lb (500 g) tomatoes, peeled and coarsely chopped

1 lb (500 g) ziti

grated locatelli cheese, for the table

Place the olive oil in a saucepan. Add the garlic and pepper. Sauté over
high heat until the garlic begins to brown. Add the parboiled broccoli,
stirring one minute, to sear on all sides, then add the sliced sausage and
sear likewise. Add the tomato and stir one minute.

Lower the heat to a slow simmer and cook covered fifteen minutes
until the tomato is soft and saucy and the broccoli is well cooked.

Cook the pasta until tender. Drain and toss with the broccoli and
sausage.

Serve with grated locatelli cheese.

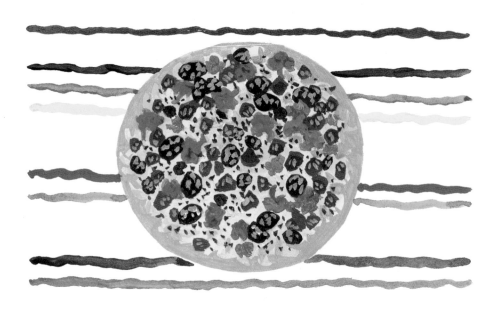

57
Rigatoni with Sausage and Peppers
Rigatoni con Salsiccia e Peperoni

Again, this is a meaty version of a vegetarian recipe (41). This sauce is a great favorite, every bit as interesting on a "hero" sandwich as it is on a plate of macaroni. For the sweetest results, we use fennel sausage, yellow onions, and red peppers, but using hot sausage or mixing the two can create interesting counter tastes. Red, orange, and green peppers with purple onions give the dish a party color.

> ½ teaspoon crushed red pepper
> ½ cup (125 ml) olive oil
> 2 cups (375 g) onion, cut in wide strips
> 2 lb (1 kg) sweet peppers, about 4 to 6, roasted (see page 80), cut into rigatoni-sized strips
> 1 lb (500 g) sausage, (approximately 4 large links), cooked and sliced (see page 101)
> 1 lb (500 g) tomatoes, peeled and chopped
> 1 lb (500 g) rigatoni
> grated locatelli cheese, for the table

Heat the crushed pepper in the olive oil, add the onion, and sauté over medium heat five minutes until soft and transparent. Add the roast peppers and stir until they are well coated with oil, about two minutes. Add the sliced sausage and sauté one minute. Now add the tomatoes. Stir briefly. Cover and cook over low heat fifteen minutes.

Bring the pasta water to a boil and add the rigatoni. Cook until *al dente* and drain. Toss with the tomato-sausage mixture. Let sit on a warm stove a minute or two until the juices are absorbed by the pasta. Serve with grated locatelli cheese.

58
Rigatoni with Sausage and Cannellini Beans
Salsiccie e Fagioli al'Capone

In our family album, there are newspaper clippings that tell an amusing story about our Granduncle Louie and his glorious, but short-lived, career as an insurance agent, selling life insurance for one of the big name Connecticut insurers. Louie's sales figures were some of the best ever for a new agent, and his policies were written for astronomical sums. He was given a commendation and a bonus. Then some underwriters at the home office in Hartford realized exactly where Louie was finding so many takers. It seems he was selling life insurance to well-known mobsters and racketeers, boys who were under fire from the police as well as one another. The policies were canceled and Uncle Louie was fired. The last policy he wrote was for Al Capone. This recipe was given to us by our dear, garrulous, enterprising uncle who swore he got it from Big Al himself. We believe him. Simple pork and beans and pasta is the kind of stick-to-your-ribs meal a man who lived as if every day could be his last might enjoy.

½ teaspoon crushed red pepper

1 clove garlic, crushed

⅓ cup (85 ml) olive oil

1 cup (185 g) onion, sliced

1 lb (500 g) sausage, approximately 4 large links, fennel, sweet, hot, or any combination, cooked and sliced (see page 101)

1½ cups (280 g) cannellini beans, canned or cooked (see pages 81 and 89)

¾ lb (375 g) tomatoes, peeled and coarsely chopped

10 large basil leaves

1 lb (500 g) rigatoni

grated Parmesan cheese, for the table

Put the pepper and garlic into the oil over medium heat for a moment, then add the sliced onion. Sauté, stirring until the onion is soft and transparent, about five minutes. Add the cooked, sliced sausage. Sauté about one minute. Add beans, tomatoes, and basil. Stir and bring to a boil. Lower the heat and simmer slowly twenty minutes, letting the flavors mix.

Cook the rigatoni. Drain. Toss with the pork and beans. Serve with grated Parmesan cheese.

59
Linguine with Sausage and Tomato Sauce
Linguine e Salsiccia Sugo di Pomodoro

For this recipe, we recommend using *cervellata* which is a thin specialty sausage, usually pork mixed with lamb and sometimes parsley, spinach, or cheese. Since it is thinner than standard sausages, we boil it a minute or two, then put it under the hot broiler three to five minutes, until brown, before we cut it into rounds.

> 1 lb (500 g) cervellata, cooked (see page 101) and sliced on the diagonal as thin as possible, keeping the cylindrical integrity of the sausage
> 1½ lb (750 g) plum tomatoes, peeled and quartered
> 6 oz (185 g) tomato paste
> ¼ cup (30 g) Italian parsley, finely chopped
> 15 basil leaves
> 1 teaspoon dried oregano
> ½ cup (125 ml) olive oil
> 1 large clove garlic, pressed or finely chopped
> ½ teaspoon crushed red pepper
> 1 lb (500 g) linguine
> grated locatelli cheese, for the table

Prepare the sausage and place in a bowl with the tomatoes, tomato paste, parsley, basil, and oregano.

Put the oil in a saucepan with the garlic and pepper flakes over a high flame. When the garlic begins to brown and the pepper burns slightly, add the tomato mixture. Sizzle and stir until everything is thoroughly mixed.

Reduce the heat to simmer, cover and continue cooking, five minutes if you like your tomatoes firm, fifteen minutes or longer if you like a smooth sauce.

Cook the pasta. Drain when slightly underdone. Toss with half the sauce, saving the rest to spoon on top. Serve with grated locatelli cheese.

Chicken
Pollo

Uncle Sal was our hero, and we looked forward to our poultry delivery days just to see him. Even though he was born in Palermo and was three when he moved here with our grandparents on our mother's side, he was a Yankee Doodle through and through. As a fighter pilot stationed in Italy during World War II, he proved he was no chicken. He was a do-or-die guy, not a man to flinch an inch. He returned from the war with a medal of honor and a metal plate in his head. We are not sure which was the cause, his injury, his exposure to the encrustation of decadence and privilege in Italy, or a feeling of brotherhood and common purpose with the men in his squadron, but the feather in his cap might as well have been macaroni. The postwar Uncle Sal was an atheist and interested in the Communist Party. He wanted to go out west and organize farm workers and even wanted to visit Moscow.

Of course this led to a serious conflict with Grandpa who, while he allowed his son freedom of religion, expected him to man the cleaver in the family private enterprise: Corsi and Son Live Poultry. In the end, father was tougher than son. Grandpa won, but died shortly after, leaving Sal, married with children, in charge. Sal joined the business and spent his life in Brooklyn filling orders for restaurants and catering halls. He was a lot freer with the hens than Grandpa, however, and we were never at a loss for chickens and ducks. We had eggs on tap like water. Uncle Sal remains an ultraliberal to this day, supplying poultry at cost or free of charge not only to family, but to friends and anyone whose ability to pay is less than his need.

Although you can use leftover chicken to make the recipes that follow (and there was never a shortage of it in our house), they are written to be made from scratch. Mixed with a pound (500 g) of pasta, a pound (500 g) of chicken will serve four as a main course.

We prefer to start with boneless, skinless chicken breasts and thighs. We trim them of excess fat, slice them into bite-sized pieces, and marinate them in balsamic or wine vinegar at least one hour before cooking to tenderize and sweeten.

60
Rigatoni with Chicken and Roast Peppers
Rigatoni con Pollo e Pimenti

This is, like the sausage and peppers recipe, a meaty version of recipe 41. Our experience in the kitchen has taught us what a difference one ingredient can make. Chicken brings out the lightness of the peppers, whereas the sausage accents their heartiness.

>1 lb (500 g) chicken, boneless, skinless, cut into rectangles, 1 by 2 inches (2.5 by 5 cm)
>
>¼ cup (60 ml) balsamic or wine vinegar
>
>½ cup (125 ml) olive oil
>
>1 cup (185 g) onion, cut into large wedges
>
>2 lb (1 kg) sweet peppers (about 4 to 6) in assorted colors, roasted and skinned (see page 80), cut 1 by 2 inches (2.5 by 5 cm)
>
>½ teaspoon crushed red pepper
>
>1 lb (500 g) tomatoes, peeled and cut into large slices
>
>1 lb (500 g) rigatoni
>
>grated Parmesan or Romano cheese, for the table

Marinate chicken in vinegar at least one hour. Heat ¼ cup (60 ml) of the olive oil and add the onion. Sauté over medium-high heat until the onion is soft and transparent, about five minutes. Add the peppers, stir briefly, cover, and place on low heat fifteen minutes.

In another saucepan, heat the remaining ¼ cup (60 ml) of oil and the red pepper flakes. Add the marinated chicken and sear on high heat, stirring constantly about one minute. Add the tomatoes and stir one minute. Lower heat, add the peppers and onion from the other pot, mix well, cover, and cook all the ingredients together an additional five minutes.

Cook the rigatoni then drain. Return to the pot and toss with the chicken and peppers.

Serve with the grated Parmesan or Romano cheese.

61
Orzo with Chicken, Pine Nuts, and Mushrooms
Orzo con Pignoli e Fungi

Sunday nights were "Chinese" nights at the Corsi's. The clan wanted something light after the heavy afternoon lunch. While the men played cards and the kids watched TV, the aunts would throw together whatever vegetables and meat were left over with a rice-shaped macaroni called *orzo* (or *riso* as it is also known). The food wasn't fancy like risotto, it was anything and everything: chicken, beef, veal, pork, shrimp, scallops, peas, mushrooms, almonds, chestnuts, onions, a can of tuna or clams. Sometimes we even put soy sauce on it. Here is a fresh, start-from-scratch example of that hodgepodge we still find enjoyable. Make whatever substitutions you wish.

> 1 lb (500 g) boneless chicken, cut into strips ½ by 1 inch (1 by 2.5 cm)
>
> ¼ cup (60 ml) balsamic or wine vinegar
>
> ¼ cup (60 g) pine nuts
>
> ½ lb (250 g) shiitake mushrooms
>
> 3 tablespoons (45 g) butter
>
> ½ cup (125 ml) olive oil
>
> 1 clove garlic, peeled
>
> ¼ teaspoon crushed red pepper
>
> ¼ cup (30 g) Italian parsley, chopped
>
> 1 cup (185 g) shelled peas
>
> 1 lb (500 g) orzo

Marinate chicken in vinegar one hour.

Toast the pine nuts in a heavy pan over high heat, shaking or stirring constantly so that they brown evenly. Remove from pan and set aside.

Clean the mushrooms well. Remove tough stems and slice the caps and remaining stems into ¼ inch (5 mm) strips.

Melt butter ¼ cup (60 ml) in the olive oil. Add the whole garlic clove. Add the mushrooms and sauté until almost soft. Remove them from the pan with the butter-oil mixture and keep warm. Discard the garlic clove.

Place the red pepper and the remaining ¼ cup (60 ml) olive oil in a large pan. When the oil is hot, add the chicken, quickly stir-frying about three minutes. Add the pine nuts. Stir thirty seconds longer. Add the cooked mushrooms, parsley, and peas. Remove from the heat but keep warm.

Cook the orzo. Before it is *al dente*, drain. Reheat the other ingredients and add the orzo. Stir-fry quickly, mixing well for an additional two minutes. Let sit a minute to absorb the juices before serving.

62

Linguine with Chicken, Sausage, and Green Olives
Pollo Scapariello

When making this recipe, we prefer to use chicken thighs and fennel
sausage, but on more than one occasion we have enjoyed it with the
breasts and hot sausage. For more meaty fun, we sometimes add a few
chicken livers. It's delicious if you have a taste for them.
Once again, whether you use dark or white meat or a combination of
both, use boneless, skinless chicken. Cut the meat into small cubes
and marinate several hours ahead of time in ¼ cup (60 ml) of balsamic
vinegar.
This dish can be quite good with novelty sausages, especially the
thinner specialty ones stuffed with cheese and parsley, spinach, and so
forth. In some Italian meat markets, cooked sausage is available.
Otherwise, cook the sausage as in recipes (56) to (59).

1 lb (500 g) boned, skinned chicken, diced ¾ inch (2 cm)
¼ cup (60 ml) balsamic or wine vinegar
½ lb (250 g) sausage, cooked and sliced(see page 101)
½ teaspoon crushed red pepper
1 cup (185 g) onion, minced
½ cup (125 ml) olive oil
4 chicken livers, finely chopped (optional)
¾ lb (375 g) tomatoes, peeled and chopped
10 oil-cured Sicilian green olives, pitted and finely chopped
1 lb (500 g) linguine
grated locatelli or Parmesan cheese, for the table

Prepare chicken and marinate in vinegar several hours. Cook sausage.
Heat the pepper and onion in the olive oil. Cook over medium heat
about five minutes, stirring constantly until onion is transparent.
Add the chicken (and chicken livers if you are using them), raise the
heat, and continue to sauté until the meat is cooked through, about two
or three minutes.
Add the precooked sausage slices, stir a minute, then add the tomatoes
and olives. Simmer on low heat another five minutes.
Cook pasta until tender, drain, and toss with the other ingredients.
Serve with grated locatelli or Parmesan cheese.

63
Spaghetti with Chicken and Rosemary
Spaghetti con Pollo Rosmarino

Whenever the subject is chicken, the name *Uncle Sal* pops up. A populist at heart, Sal had a liking for the pedestrian in food. Because of his princely spirit in business, he was treated like a guest at many superior Italian restaurants in the five boroughs and tasted some of the finest poultry dishes, but he preferred ordinary fried chicken cutlets. He invented a thing called a *Chicken Pop*, a boon to humanity which his politics prohibited him from patenting. In the spirit of a corn dog, it was a piece of breaded boneless chicken impaled on a stick and deep-fried. He was, however, partial to chicken and rosemary.

The chicken in this dish is sweet, but also slightly sour, and should be more tender than the pasta. (Remember *al dente* when cooking the pasta!) Adding the currants and rosemary to the marinade and then sautéing them along with the chicken infuses their flavor deeply into the meat and gives this dish a unique piquancy.

1 lb (500 g) chicken, boned, skinned, cut into strips ½ by 2 inches (1 by 5 cm)

¼ cup (60 ml) wine vinegar

1 teaspoon grated lemon rind

2 tablespoons currants

4 tablespoons rosemary

2 tablespoons pine nuts

¾ teaspoon crushed red pepper

½ cup (125 ml) olive oil

½ lb (250 g) tomatoes, peeled and chopped

1 lb (500 g) spaghetti

Marinate the chicken strips in the vinegar, lemon rind, currants, and rosemary at least two hours.

Toast the pine nuts in a pan over medium heat until brown and set aside.

Heat the crushed red pepper in the olive oil over high heat.

Just before it smokes, add the chicken, along with the marinade. Stir until the meat is braised on all sides, about one or two minutes.

Add the tomatoes and pine nuts; stir thirty seconds. Lower heat, cover, and simmer slowly ten minutes until the tomatoes are soft.

Cook the pasta, drain, and toss with other ingredients.

64
Fettuccine with Chicken Livers
Fegato di Pollo con Fettuccine

Chicken giblets always came along with the delivery from Uncle Sal.

½ lb (250 g) chicken livers, sliced in thirds
1 tablespoon lemon juice
⅓ cup (85 ml) plus 1 tablespoon (15 ml) olive oil
¼ lb (125 g) pancetta thickly sliced then diced ¼ inch (5 mm)
1 lb (500 g) fettucine
1 tablespoon (15 g) sweet butter
½ teaspoon crushed red pepper
15 sage leaves _or_ (1 teaspoon dried)
1 teaspoon thyme
¼ cup (30 g) finely chopped Italian parsley

Mix the livers with lemon juice and set aside.

Place 1 tablespoon (15 ml) of the olive oil in a pan, add the pancetta, and sauté until crisp over medium heat, stirring constantly, about five or ten minutes. Remove from the pan and set aside. Pour off any bacon grease.

Start cooking the fettuccine.

Melt the butter in ⅓ cup (85 ml) of the olive oil over medium-high heat. Add the red pepper and the chicken livers. Fry on one side, then the other, one to two minutes, or until the liver is cooked. Sprinkle in the pancetta bits, stir, then add the sage, thyme, and parsley. Mix well.

Turn off the heat, cover, and keep warm while you finish cooking the fettucine.

Drain the fettucine and toss with the chicken livers.

Duck
Anitra

Peking ducks—or must we now say *Beijing?*—were imported from China years ago and are the most commonly available. They have been cultivated in America and Europe for centuries and weigh in at about five pounds (2½ Kg). Also known as Long Island ducks, they tend to be juicier and milder than the wild varieties, which can be tough and gamey.

A much less frequent visitor to the table than chicken, duck can offer a welcome change. The meat is quite rich and its presence in a dish can make a meal seem a more festive occasion. This is not due to the fact that duck is especially costly or rare, but that its preparation time is longer than that of chicken.

Ducks must be roasted before being used in these recipes. Place uncovered bird in a roasting pan in a 325° F (170° C/gas 3) oven for three hours. Pour off fat every forty minutes. Let cool. Peel away and discard the skin, then carve the breast and thigh meat from the bone and cut into bite-sized pieces. (Legs and wings have little or no edible meat.) The liver sautéed briefly in a little oil may also be added to the following recipes.

65
Spaghetti with Duck, Fennel, and Orange
Spaghetti Vindicare

Potent, but with the richness of the duck cut by the tangy bitterness of the radicchio and toned down by the sweet digestibility of the fennel, it becomes balanced for all its complexity. A thoroughly delectable dish.

> 5 lb (2½ kg) duck, (see page 112 for preparation)
> 2 tablespoons balsamic vinegar
> ½ cup (125 ml) olive oil
> 1 teaspoon crushed red pepper
> ½ cup (90 g) chopped shallots (spring onions)
> 1 bulb fennel, cleaned (see page 73) and the small inner bulb finely chopped
> 1 lb (500 g) spaghetti
> 1 head radicchio (4 oz/125 g) cut slaw-style
> 1 tablespoon finely grated orange rind
> 2 tablespoons chopped parsley
> 2 tablespoons red wine
> 6 oz (185 g) tomato paste

In a bowl, toss the duck meat with the vinegar.

Heat the olive oil with the red pepper in a heavy pot. Add the shallots and sauté about three minutes over medium-high heat. Add the fennel and sauté two minutes longer.

In separate pot, begin to boil the spaghetti.

Meanwhile, add the radicchio, orange rind, and parsley to the shallot fennel mixture. Stir-fry one minute. Add the wine, then the duck and the tomato paste mixed with ½ cup (125 ml) water. Mix thoroughly. Turn off heat, cover and let stand while the pasta finishes cooking.

Before draining the pasta, reserve another ½ cup (125 ml) water. Toss with the sauce, using the reserved water if needed to help distribute the ingredients evenly.

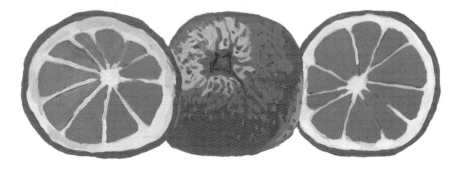

66
Orzo with Duck
Orzo all'Anitra

Pork and duck. Calling all carnivores.

5 lb (2½ kg) duck (see page 112 for preparation)
1 tablespoon thyme
2 tablespoons balsamic vinegar
1 tablespoon (15 g) butter
¼ cup (60 ml) olive oil
2 cloves garlic, pressed or minced
1 tablespoon hot chili pepper sliced thin (or ¾ teaspoon crushed red pepper)
1 cup (185 g) purple (Spanish) onion, chopped in small pieces
1 lb (500 g) tomatoes, peeled and chopped in small pieces
½ lb (250 g) pork sausage, (three or four links), cooked and sliced (see page 101)
½ cup (125 ml) white wine
1 lb (500 g) orzo, or riso

In a bowl, mix the thyme with the prepared duck and add the vinegar.

In a large (12″ or 30 cm) frying pan, melt the butter in the olive oil. Add the garlic, pepper, and onion and sauté over medium-high heat for about three minutes.

Boil the orzo for four minutes.

Meanwhile, add the tomatoes and the sausage rounds to the frying pan and simmer lightly over medium heat for one minute.

Drain the orzo through a strainer, reserving one cup of the water it was boiled in. Lower the heat under the frying pan. Add the orzo, the reserved water, and the wine to the pan and mix thoroughly. Mix in the duck. Cover and simmer for about twenty minutes over low heat until the orzo is cooked and all juices and liquids are absorbed.

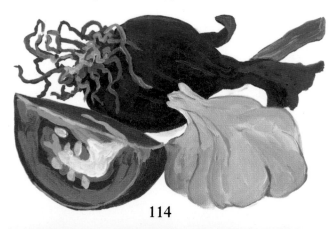

Beef
Manzo

In typical European noodle and beef dishes, stews, goulashes, hashes, stroganoffs, and such, the beef is cut in chunks and strips. Like hamburger-eating Americans, southern Italians prefer their beef ground. Perhaps this is the reason why, in America, "spaghetti and meatballs" has such a familiar ring to it.

Come hell or high water, we always had meat sauce on Sunday. We remember family picnics at Hempstead State Park. While everyone else in the park grilled franks, chicken, and burgers over charcoal, our mothers boiled meat sauce and pasta *al fresco* on an open wood fire in the cinder-block grill which the state provided for each picnic table. Under the oaks by the lake, we sat and ate macaroni with meat sauce.

If you plan to add meatballs to the basic meat sauce, cut the amount of beef for the sauce in half. The following recipes will make a dozen meatballs.

Meatballs
Polpette

2 tablespoons (30 g) butter

2 tablespoons olive oil

½ teaspoon crushed red pepper

1 cup (185 g) onions, finely chopped

1 lb (500 g) ground beef (or a mixture of one-half ground
beef, one-quarter ground pork, and one-quarter ground
veal)

2 eggs

½ cup (60 g) bread crumbs

¼ cup (60 ml) red wine

¼ cup (30 g) Italian parsley, finely chopped

¼ cup (30 g) grated locatelli cheese

12 raisins (optional)

12 pine nuts (optional)

½ cup (125 ml) olive oil, for frying

Melt the butter in the oil over medium heat. Add the pepper and onion
and sauté about five minutes, or until the onion is soft and transparent.

Combine the meat, eggs, bread crumbs, sautéed onions, wine, parsley, and cheese in a large bowl and mix thoroughly.

Divide the mixture into twelve rounds, putting one raisin and one pine
nut in each, if you wish. Form them into meatballs. It helps to rub your
palms with a little olive oil when rolling the meatballs.

Put the olive oil in an 8-inch (20-cm) frying pan and fry the meatballs,
turning until golden brown. Now the meatballs are ready to be simmered
in meat sauce. Follow the next recipe (page 117).

67
Spaghetti with Meat Sauce
Spaghetti Normalità

Because of the popularity of new kinds of pasta sauces, basic meat sauce has fallen out of favor. It is, however, like the meatballs above, still a favorite among more traditional eaters. We are filled with respect for the dish, for as Italian Americans, it is the pasta on which we cut our eyeteeth—our graduation from pastina and butter to "real food."

1 tablespoon (15 g) butter

⅓ cup (85 ml) olive oil

½ teaspoon crushed red pepper

2 cloves garlic, pressed or minced

1 cup (185 g) onion, finely chopped

1 lb (500 g) ground sirloin (use half this amount if you add
  the meatballs described above)

2 lb (1 kg) tomatoes, peeled, with their juice

6 oz (185 g) tomato paste

¼ cup (30 g) Italian parsley, finely chopped

25 large basil leaves

½ teaspoon dried oregano

1 lb (500 g) spaghetti

grated locatelli cheese for the table

Melt the butter in the oil over medium heat. Add the pepper, garlic, and onion and sauté five minutes, or until the onion is soft and transparent.

Raise the heat. Add the beef and sauté, stirring constantly until the meat is brown all over, about five minutes at medium-high heat. Lower the heat a bit if the meat starts sticking.

Add the tomatoes, with their juices, tomato paste, parsley, basil, and oregano. Stir thoroughly while bringing to a boil. Then lower the heat (add the fried meatballs at this time), cover, and simmer forty minutes to thicken the sauce.

Cook the spaghetti. After draining, return it to the pot and add 1 cup (250 ml) of the meat sauce, mixing well to keep the spaghetti from sticking or getting too hard and wiry.

To serve, put a portion of spaghetti in each bowl and pour a ladle of sauce on top with a meatball or two, if you are serving them. The remaining sauce should be placed on the table.

Serve with grated locatelli cheese.

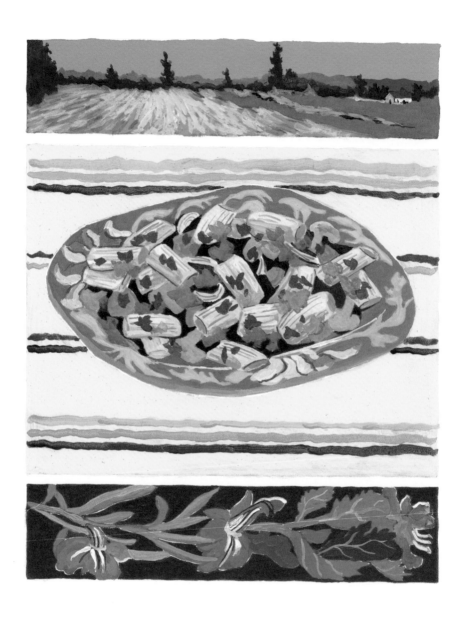

Veal
Vitello

Veal is young beef, six months to a year old. Although veal needs no tenderizing, we recommend marinating it. As with chicken and duck, a small amount of vinegar mellows it and adds a dimension to its somewhat mild flavor.

68
Rigatoni with Veal and Mushrooms
Pasta con Vitello e Fungi

Here is a basic recipe for veal and mushrooms in a wine sauce. Of the gourmet varieties of mushrooms currently available, we like shiitake mushrooms best. Be careful: sometimes the stems are tough. If you use the meatier portabellos, you will probably need to stir-fry the mushrooms a minute or two longer to wilt them. If you use dried porcinis, start with three or four ounces [90 to 125 g] and reconstitute them in white wine twenty-five minutes. They make this dish earthy. We recommend making this in a large frying pan, especially if you use portabellos, which are bulky and take up a lot of room before cooking.

> 1 lb (500 g) veal cutlets, cut in short thin strips
> ¼ cup (60 ml) balsamic or wine vinegar
> 2 tablespoons (30 g) sweet butter
> ½ cup (125 ml) olive oil
> ½ teaspoon crushed red pepper
> 1 cup (185 g) onion, chopped
> 1 lb (500 g) mushrooms, caps cut into strips
> 2 tablespoons finely chopped Italian parsley
> 10 large basil leaves
> 1 teaspoon dried rosemary
> ¼ cup (60 ml) white wine
> 1 lb (500 g) rigatoni
> grated locatelli cheese, for the table

Marinate veal in vinegar one hour or longer.

Over medium heat using a large pan or wok, melt the butter in the oil, add the crushed red pepper and the onion, and sauté five minutes until the onion is soft.

Raise heat to high, add the mushrooms, and quickly stir-fry about one minute. Keep the heat turned up and add the veal. Stir-fry for two minutes more.

Add the parsley, basil, rosemary, and wine, lower heat, cover, and cook over low heat another five minutes.

Cook the pasta until done. Toss with the veal and mushrooms and serve with grated locatelli cheese.

Lamb
Agnello

In Greece, and throughout points further east, lamb occupies a much greater place in the diet than does beef, and this is true in parts of Sicily where the Old Ways still linger. Like fish, traditional on Christmas Eve, lamb is more than a meat; it is a symbol for the Lord and is often served as one of the courses at the Easter Feast.
We find that the best and leanest ground lamb is from the leg.

69
Ground Lamb and Eggplant Lasagna
Lasagna al'Agnello e Melanzane

Once upon a time, in the not-so-distant past, lasagna was very popular. But when the trend turned away from red meat to lighter fare and shorter cooking times, many of these baked, layered pasta recipes fell into obscurity. We have included several lasagna recipes, hoping to inspire a renaissance of those simpler, more relaxed times when Sunday dinner was a long, drawn-out event, and the family took the opportunity to share one day a week arguing, cooking, and eating. This recipe, a Sicilian relation of moussaka, shows Greek influence. The following recipe will fill a baking dish measuring 9 by 11 by 3 inches (22 by 28 by 7 cm) and serve six to eight.

1 tablespoon (15 g) butter
⅓ cup (85 ml) olive oil
½ teaspoon crushed red pepper
1 cup (185 g) onion, minced
2 cloves garlic
1 lb (500 g) ground leg of lamb
35 oz (1 kg) canned peeled tomatoes, with juice
6 oz (185 g) tomato paste
¼ cup (30 g) Italian parsley
25 large basil leaves

1 teaspoon rosemary

2 lb (1 kg) eggplant (aubergine), sliced ¼ inch (5 mm)
  (see page 24)

¾ cup (185 ml) olive oil, for frying

2 eggs, beaten

1 lb (500 g) ricotta cheese

6 oz (185 g) goat cheese (Montrachet, for example)

1 teaspoon grated nutmeg

1 lb (500 g) lasagna

¼ cup (30 g) grated locatelli cheese

Preheat the oven to 375° F (190° C/gas 5).

Melt the butter in the olive oil in your saucepot. Add the red pepper, onion, and garlic and sauté over high heat three minutes, stirring constantly. Add the lamb and braise the meat another five minutes, stirring constantly. Add the tomatoes and their juice, the tomato paste, parsley, basil, and rosemary to the lamb mixture. Lower the heat, cover, and simmer twenty minutes, stirring occasionally.

Meanwhile, fry the eggplant slices and in hot oil until they are brown on both sides. Remove with a slotted spoon and set aside, saving the oil.

Combine the eggs, ricotta, goat cheese, and nutmeg in a bowl and mix thoroughly.

Bring pasta water to a boil. Add a tablespoon of the oil you used to fry the eggplant to the pasta water to keep the lasagna from sticking. Boil the lasagna four to five minutes, or until it is half done. Drain the lasagna and add cold water to the pot so that you can handle the noodles.

Swab the sides and bottom of your baking dish with some of the eggplant oil. (Refrigerate what remains of this oil; you can use it in the future for frying or sautéing meat or vegetables.) Put one quarter of the tomato-sauce on the bottom of the baking dish. Lay down a third of the lasagna noodles, overlapping them and running them up the sides of the dish. Spoon another quarter of the sauce over them. Place half the eggplant on top of that, followed by half the ricotta cheese–egg mixture spread as evenly as possible. A metal spoon dipped in cold water will help.

Repeat the layering process with one third of the noodles, another quarter of the sauce, the remaining half of the eggplant, and the remaining cheese mixture. Finish with the rest of lasagna, and cover the top with the remaining sauce. Sprinkle the locatelli cheese evenly across the top.

Cover well and bake forty minutes. Uncover and bake another ten minutes. Remove from the oven and let sit thirty minutes before serving. Don't be in a hurry. Sitting gives the lasagna a chance to set. This is the perfect time to have a glass of wine in anticipation of a great meal.

70
Acini di Pepe with Lamb, Chickpeas, Herbs, and Vegetables
Casserola d'Agnello

This dish certainly shows Middle Eastern influence. *Acini di pepe* is a grain-shaped pasta, slightly larger and firmer than couscous. It is partially cooked first and then steamed on top of the spicy sauce. The following recipe will serve six to eight.

1 lb (500 g) acini di pepe
¾ cup (185 ml) olive oil
2 cloves garlic, pressed or minced
1 teaspoon crushed red pepper
1 cup (185 g) onion, chopped ¼ inch (5 mm)
1½ lbs (750 g) ground leg of lamb
1 cup (185 g) celery, chopped ¼ inch (5 mm)
1 cup (185 g) carrot, chopped ¼ inch (5 mm)
1 cup (200 g) potato, chopped ¼ inch (5 mm)
1½ lb (750 g) tomatoes, peeled and chopped
1 cup (250 ml) white wine
1 tablespoon rosemary
1 tablespoon thyme
1 teaspoon ground cumin
1 teaspoon ground coriander
1 teaspoon ground sage
2 cups (375 g) cooked chickpeas, (see page 86) or 19 oz (550 g) canned and drained
¼ cup (30 g) Italian parsley, finely chopped

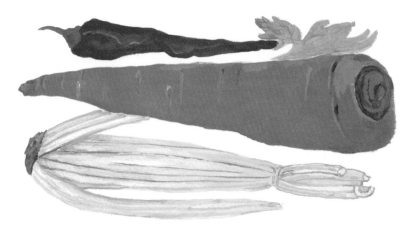

Parboil the acini di pepe in 6 quarts (6 liters) of water three minutes. Strain. Place in a ceramic bowl, mixing it thoroughly with ¼ cup (60 ml) of the olive oil. Cover with a plate until you are ready to use.

In a large skillet with a cover, heat the garlic and pepper in the remaining ½ cup (125 ml) of olive oil. Add the onion and sauté three minutes over high heat until it softens.

Add the lamb and sauté another five minutes, stirring to braise the meat on all sides until it begins to brown. Then add the celery, carrots, and potatoes and sauté five minutes longer. Add the tomatoes, wine, and herbs, except for the parsley. Bring to a boil, then lower the heat to simmer.

Now spread the parboiled acini evenly over the top of the sauce. It should form a thin layer. Break up any clumps with your hands. Do not stir it in. You want it to steam slowly. Mix the chickpeas with the parsley and place on top of the acini.

Cover the skillet and cook forty-five minutes on low heat, or until all the liquid is absorbed and the acini is tender.

If you find the liquid evaporating before the acini is cooked, add some extra wine, or if you used canned tomatoes, the juice will do.

Ham
Prosciutto

There are several types of Italian ham. The Parma type, prosciutto, is well known for its leanness and its soft flavor. We recommend this fine imported ham for the following recipes.

71
Lasagna with Ham, Cheese, and Spinach
Lasagna Giovanni

A recent survey revealed that the ham and cheese sandwich is America's most often served meal. Here is a Sicilian recipe that is, in its way, a version of that American classic. It makes great leftovers, cold or reheated. Like most lasagna, it is very good party food. Prepared and baked ahead of time, it is almost better reheated rather than fresh from the oven.

The following recipe will fill a baking dish measuring 8 by 10 by 3 inches (20 by 25 by 7 cm) and serve six to eight.

¾ cup (185 ml) olive oil
½ teaspoon crushed red pepper
2 lb (1 kg) spinach, coarsely chopped
1½ lb (750 g) tomatoes, peeled
15 large basil leaves
2 cloves garlic, pressed or minced
2 tablespoons rosemary
1 lb (500 g) lasagna
½ lb (250 g) prosciutto, thinly sliced
½ lb (250 g) mozzarella cheese, grated
¼ cup (60 ml) grated Parmesan or Romano cheese

Preheat oven to 350° F (180° C/gas 4).

Heat ½ cup (125 ml) of the olive oil in your saucepan with the red pepper. When the oil is very hot, begin adding the spinach in handfuls, stirring until wilted. Remove from the heat and keep warm.

Place the tomatoes, basil, garlic, and rosemary with the other ¼ cup (60 ml) of olive oil in a blender or food processor and purée. You should end up with two to three cups.

Bring pasta water to a boil. Add a few drops of olive oil to keep the lasagna from sticking. Boil the noodles until *al dente* but flexible enough to work with. Pour off half the water and add cold water to stop the cooking. Let cool until you can handle them.

Spread ¼ of the tomato purée on the bottom of the baking dish. Divide the lasagna into three parts. Place a layer of lasagna on the bottom of the pan. The noodles should overlap. To make a firm, architecturally sound lasagna, pasta layers should have some cross-pieces, especially on the bottom. If some of the lasagna is broken, use it in the middle layer, saving the whole pieces for the top.

Put half the spinach on the bottom layer of lasagna, spreading evenly. Place half of the ham on top of the spinach, then add a layer of half the grated mozzarella and spread another ¼ of the tomato purée.

Add another layer of lasagna noodles and the other half of the spinach, and the other half of the ham, the other half of the mozzarella, then another ¼ of the tomato purée. Finish with a layer of noodles and top with the remaining tomato purée. Be sure to cover the lasagna well with the tomato, or the noodles will dry out and burn. Finish with a layer of grated Parmesan or Romano cheese.

Bake covered forty minutes, then uncovered ten minutes. Remove from the oven and let sit fifteen minutes to firm up before serving.

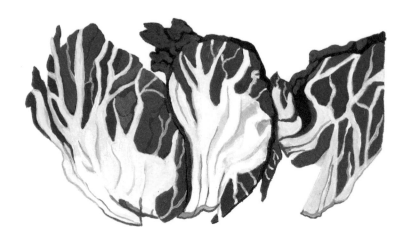

72
Linguine with Prosciutto and Radicchio
Linguine con Prosciutto Cotto e Radicchio

Radicchio, a purple-red lettuce, can be quite bitter, especially when cooked. The saltiness of the ham also seems to bring out that quality. Nevertheless, using the radicchio makes for a tasty dish with a complex flavor.

> ½ cup (125 ml) olive oil
> 6 oz (185 g) prosciutto, thickly sliced then diced ¼ inch (5 mm)
> 1 clove garlic, cut into slivers
> ¼ teaspoon crushed red pepper
> 1 tablespoon rosemary
> ¼ lb (120 g) radicchio, finely sliced
> ¼ cup (30 g) Italian parsley, finely chopped
> 1 lb (500 g) linguine
> grated Parmesan cheese, for the table

Put a tablespoon of the olive oil in your saucepan, add the prosciutto, and cook over medium heat until prosciutto is crisp, stirring constantly. This should take about five minutes. Remove the prosciutto from the pan and discard the excess fat.

Add the remaining olive oil, garlic, red pepper, and rosemary, stirring one minute over high heat. Then add the radicchio and parsley, stirring constantly half a minute. Add the prosciutto and heat for another half minute. Make sure you break up any clumps of radicchio that stick together.

Cook the linguine, drain, and toss with the radicchio-prosciutto mixture. Serve with grated Parmesan cheese.

Mixed Meats
Carne Mista

73
Baked Shells, Sicilian Style, with Pork, Beef, and Veal
Conchieglie al Forno con Carne Mista

We have enjoyed this meaty recipe in versions that are both more and
less complicated. Sometimes bits of bacon, or pancetta, are added for
flavor. Occasionally, ground lamb is used as well as the other meats. For
a lighter dish, use less meat.
Caciocavallo, a tangy sheep's milk Sicilian specialty, is not widely
available. This is unfortunate. However, other cheeses can be
substituted without harming the general intent of the dish.
Serves six to eight.

1 tablespoon (15 g) sweet butter

½ cup (125 ml) plus 3 tablespoons (30 ml) olive oil

1 cup (185 g) onion, chopped in small pieces

½ teaspoon crushed red pepper

1 clove garlic, pressed or minced

½ lb (250 g) ground pork

½ lb (250 g) ground beef

½ lb (250 g) ground veal

1½ lb (750 g) tomatoes, peeled and chopped

¼ cup (60 ml) red wine

6 oz (185 g) tomato paste

2 tablespoons Italian parsley, finely chopped

1 bay leaf

1 teaspoon dried oregano

10 large basil leaves

½ cup (60 g) bread crumbs

3 tablespoons grated locatelli cheese

1 lb (500 g) shells

10 oz (315 g) frozen peas, thawed, or shelled fresh peas, if
available

6 oz (185 g) caciocavallo cheese, coarsely grated (Asiago, or
even provolone, will do)

Melt the butter in the ½ cup (125 ml) of olive oil. Add the onion, red pepper, and garlic. Sauté over medium heat, stirring regularly five minutes, or until the onion is soft and transparent.

Add the ground meat, sauté five minutes longer, stirring constantly, until it starts to brown. Mix in the tomatoes, wine, tomato paste, parsley, bay leaf, oregano, and basil. Lower the heat, cover, and simmer slowly twenty minutes.

Preheat the oven to 375° F (190° C/gas 5).

Mix the remaining 3 tablespoons of olive oil with the bread crumbs and grated locatelli. Set aside.

Boil the pasta water and cook the pasta until it is half done. Drain and toss with about 3 cups (750 ml) of the sauce. (Save at least 1 cup (250 ml) for the bottom and top.) Add the peas, then the caciocavallo cheese. Mix thoroughly.

Spread a thin layer of sauce on the bottom of a large baking dish. Turn in the pasta mixture. Cover with a layer of sauce and top it off with the bread crumb mixture.

Bake covered twenty-five minutes, then uncovered five to ten minutes until the top is crisp and deep golden brown. Let it sit five minutes before serving. Extra sauce can be set at the table.

Variation: This dish can be made as a stew with meat chunks rather than ground meat. In this case, don't bake the dish, but boil the pasta until it is done and toss with the chunky meat sauce. Omit the bread crumb topping and serve the cheese at the table. Serve with bread to scoop up the extra sauce.

Pasta with Fish
Pesce

Because Sicily is surrounded by the Mediterranean, there are almost more recipes for pasta with seafood than there are kinds of fish. We grew up listening to tales of Sicilian fishermen returning daily in boats brimming with their fresh catch of shellfish, squid, sardines, swordfish, and tuna.

Sheepshead Bay was not that far from where we lived in Brooklyn, and Grandma Adela especially liked to go there because of all the fish heads and squid guts they gave her free with her other fish purchases. She would carry these back home and dig them into the soil to fertilize her beloved rose bushes and tomato plants.

She cooked everything from abalone to octopus, and as children we felt confident putting these monsters and their tentacles into our mouths, even though these delicacies horrified some of our non-Italian friends. Of course, these very same sea creatures have become fashionable now that *sushi* and *cucina nova* have arrived. We are long on recipes for them. The following are among our favorites, selected from the vast trove of family treasures—some new, some old.

Sardines
Sarde

*P*asta con sarde, pasta with sardines, like pasta with spaghetti and eggplant, is prepared in countless ways. We use canned sardines packed in olive oil. On a recent trip back to Sicily, we found canned sardines used in *pasta con sarde* in many restaurants, and we are losing no sleep over our endorsement of the practical. However, should you find fresh sardines, by all means use them. You'll need 1 pound (500 g) of the fillets. Although these dishes contain some surprising pot-mates, they are far more delectable than one might expect.

74
Perciatelli with Sardines and Currants
Pasta con Sarde I

Almost every recipe for this Sicilian classic bemoans the fact that the authentic ingredients are not available. It seems every cookbook writer rains on the parade by saying that the sardines must be fresh, or should you actually manage to find fresh sardines, they'll be from the wrong ocean—the Atlantic variety is supposedly inferior to those in the Tyrrhenian Sea. Recipe writers rue the obtainable fennel saying that the real thing must be wild, woody, and from the hills behind the Busambra Rock, or the saffron must be from Arabian crocuses, or the raisins must be from types of grapes not cultivated since the year 1500. We enjoy *pasta con sarde* made with ingredients available in any good supermarket with no particular sorrow. In fact, we rather enjoy pouring leftover sardine oil into the pasta water. This gives the pasta an especially nasty perfume.

3 tablespoons currants or chopped raisins
2 slices bread, to yield ½ cup (60 g) croutons
2 cans sardines (3¾ oz/105 g each) packed in olive oil
¼ teaspoon crushed red pepper, to taste (optional)
1 cup (185 g) chopped onion
½ cup (125 ml) olive oil
1 bulb of fennel, cleaned (see page 73) and chopped
3 tablespoons pine nuts
pinch saffron
4 anchovies
1 lb (500 g) perciatelli

Soak the currants in warm water for thirty minutes, then drain and set aside.

To make the croutons, toast two slices of your favorite bread and dice. Drain the sardines and reserve the oil. Place 2 tablespoons of it in a sauce pot and heat. Add the bread to the hot oil. Sauté over high heat, stirring constantly, until the cubes are golden brown, crisp, and well coated. The sardine flavor will give the croutons a unique essence. You may also add a bit of crushed red pepper if you like them spicy. Remove and set aside. If you prefer, bread crumbs may be substituted for the croutons.

Sauté the minced onion and the ¼ teaspoon of the red pepper in the olive oil over medium heat two or three minutes until the onion starts to turn transparent. Add the fennel and sauté five minutes. Then add the pine nuts, currants, saffron, and anchovies. Lower heat, cover, and continue cooking ten minutes.

Bring the pasta water to a boil and start cooking the perciatelli.

Five minutes before the pasta is done, add the sardines and toasted croutons to the sauce, mixing well. Continue to cook over low heat three minutes, or until the pasta is tender.

Drain the pasta and toss with the sauce.

75
Perciatelli with Sardines and Olives
Pasta con Sarde II

Here is another version of *pasta con sarde*. While the previous recipe uses currants and nuts, creating a subtle sweetness and contrast to the sardines and anchovies, here we have olives and parsley accenting the salty character of the sardines and the earthiness of the fennel.

½ cup (125 ml) olive oil
½ teaspoon crushed red pepper
1 bulb fennel, cleaned (see page 73) and diced ½ inch (1 cm)
2 cans sardines (3¾ oz/105 g each) packed in olive oil, drained
¼ cup (30 g) oil-cured black olives, pitted and chopped
¼ cup (30 g) Italian parsley, finely chopped
1 lb (500 g) spaghetti or perciatelli

Heat the olive oil and red pepper over high heat in your saucepan. Add the chopped fennel and lower the heat to medium. Stir until the fennel softens, about five minutes. Add the sardines. Do not expect them to stay whole. Sprinkle in the black olives and parsley. Cover and cook over low heat, five minutes or so, until you see the fennel is very tender. Add a tablespoon of pasta water now and then if the mixture seems too dry.

Cook the pasta. Drain, but reserve some of the water. Toss pasta with the mixture, adding water a tablespoon at a time until the pasta has a slippery coating. This dish should be moist, but not watery.

Clams
Vongole

76
Linguine with White Clam Sauce
Linguine al Vongole

This is the queen of pasta and seafood dishes.
Most fish stores will shuck clams for you if you call and order ahead of time. This will save you time and, if you are not experienced with a knife, your fingers. Make sure you tell the fishmonger you want the

clams in a container with the juice. Forget the shells unless you're short on ashtrays. We find them an annoying affectation when added to the sauce. Cherrystone clams seem to be the most satisfying for this recipe, for both flavor and texture. If they are not available, you may substitute littlenecks, but you will need to increase the amount as they are smaller and contain less juice. Probably about three dozen will do it. Chowder clams will not work. They are too tough.

18 cherrystone clams, shucked, with the juice
½ cup (60 g) Italian parsley, finely chopped
25 basil leaves
½ teaspoon dried oregano
⅓ cup (85 ml) olive oil
¾ teaspoon crushed red pepper
2 cloves garlic, pressed or minced
1 lb (500 g) linguine

Using a strainer, separate the juice from the clams, reserving the juice. Frisk the clams for pieces of shell and sand. (It is worthwhile being picky about sand. You might want to filter the clam juice through some cheesecloth or muslin. At the same time, be aware that poorly washed parsley is a more common source of grit.)

If the clams are large, cut them down to ¾ inch (2cm) pieces, feeling for bits of broken shell. Set the cut clams aside. Place in the refrigerator if you are proceeding slowly.

Measure out 1 cup (250 ml) of the reserved clam juice. Place in a large bowl and add the parsley, basil, and oregano.

Heat the oil with the red pepper and garlic until it is sizzling hot before adding the clam juice herb mixture. It is an essential part of the flavor of this dish that the oil be almost smoking hot when you add the clam juice. Stir, bring to a boil over high heat, then cover and simmer over low heat fifteen minutes.

Add the remaining clam juice to your pasta water, bring the pasta water to a boil, and add the linguine. At the same time, add the chopped clams to the broth, raise the heat, and bring the broth to a boil around the clams. Turn off the heat immediately. The clams should not boil or they may become tough, but do keep them warm.

In this recipe the pasta should be significantly underdone because it needs to absorb a good amount of liquid. Cook until three-quarters done or less. Drain and toss with the clam sauce. The absorption will take ten minutes, maybe longer. Be patient. Have some wine. Stir occasionally so that the pasta absorbs the juice evenly. If there seems to be too much liquid to absorb, or the pasta is getting cool, you may warm, stirring occasionally, over low heat fifteen or thirty seconds at a time and just before serving. This dish ready to eat only when all the liquid is absorbed.

Mussels
Cozze

77
Mussels Marinara
Cozze Marinara

When we were kids, a trip to any bay beach would provide our family with enough mussels for an impromptu picnic. Clumps of mussels were everywhere and in great abundance. Alas, this is no longer the case. In recent years, mussels have become an endangered species. Whereas we used to harvest them in Manhattan Beach, Brooklyn, the best mussels are now grown on farms, shipped from as far away as New Zealand. These are large, usually of uniform size, with blue-black shells, and very clean as they are grown in a controlled environment. If these are not available, we suggest buying mussels only in a reliable seafood shop, but you will have to clean and scrub them thoroughly and remove their beards.

4 lb (2 kg) mussels, in the shell
½ cup (125 ml) white wine
6 oz (185 g) tomato paste
1 lb (500 g) tomatoes, peeled and chopped
40 large basil leaves, (1 tablespoon, dried)
¼ cup (30 g) Italian parsley, chopped finely
¾ teaspoon dried oregano
¾ teaspoon crushed red pepper
2 cloves garlic, pressed or minced
½ cup (125 ml) olive oil
1 lb (500 g) linguine

Scrub the mussels clean and remove the seaweed beards. Pour the wine in a large pot. Add the mussels, turn up the heat, cover, and steam them open, stirring often to insure they all open fully. When they are cool enough to handle, remove the shells, catching the juice in the pot with the wine. Set the shelled mussels aside or refrigerate if it's hot in the kitchen.

Without disturbing the sediment, measure ½ cup (125 ml) of the mussel-wine liquid and mix it in a bowl with the tomato paste. It should form a thick, briny sauce.

Add tomatoes, basil, parsley, and oregano. Everything should be in a bowl together, ready to strike when the oil is hot.

Now, in your sauce pot, heat the pepper and the garlic in the olive oil. When the oil is sizzling hot, add the sauce. We like to see a big, fragrant, steamy explosion. Bring to a boil, lower the heat, and simmer fifteen

minutes to thicken. If the sauce seems watery, add a teaspoon or two of tomato paste.

Put the rest of the mussel-wine liquid in your pasta water, careful to omit any grit or sand that might have accumulated at the bottom of the pot.

Bring the pasta water to a boil and add the linguine. While the pasta is cooking, add the mussels to the sauce, raise the heat, and bring to a boil. As soon as it boils, turn off the heat. It is important not to overcook the mussels.

When the linguine is tender, drain and return to the pot. Add a ladle of sauce to the pasta and mix well to keep the pasta from becoming dry and wiry. It should be slippery. Serve with a ladle of mussel sauce on top. This is one of the few dishes where the bulk of sauce is best sitting on top.

Variations: You can make this seafood marinara with shrimp, lobster, clams, or any combination of these. Clams in red sauce would be the most common variation. Follow this recipe, substituting 18 cherrystone clams for the mussels. Whether you have the clams opened or open them yourself, save the juice and mix it with the tomato paste. Littleneck clams should be left whole, but cherrystones should be cut in two or even smaller.

When using lobster or shrimp, there will be no liquid to thin down the tomato paste. Simply use more tomatoes or a dash of wine. Have the shellfish ready, cut bite-sized, and simmer about two minutes until firm and tender. Overcooking shellfish can make it tough.

Scallops
Cannestrelli

78
Spaghettini with Scallops and Goat Cheese
Spaghettini con Cannestrelli e Formagio

Here is a tasty dish from the Siracusa area which shows some French influence. We recommend using bay scallops, which are smaller and usually sweeter than sea scallops. For the cheese, we suggest using Montrachet or a similar, tangy goat cheese, which will melt completely into the sauce.

1 lb (500 g) spaghettini

½ cup (125 ml) olive oil

½ teaspoon crushed red pepper

2 large cloves garlic, pressed or minced

1 lb (500 g) bay scallops, large scallops cut to no longer than ½ inch (1 cm)

1 lb (500 g) tomatoes, peeled and chopped into small pieces

¼ lb (125 g) oil-cured sun-dried tomatoes, coarsely chopped, with the oil

¼ cup (30 g) Italian parsley, finely chopped

6 oz (185 g) goat cheese, crumbled

This dish is made very quickly. When all the ingredients are prepared, bring your pasta water to a boil and add the pasta.

Heat the oil, pepper, and garlic over high heat. When the oil is very hot, add the scallops. Stir-fry quickly, thirty to forty seconds. Remove the scallops with a slotted spoon, letting the oil drain back into the pan.

With the heat still high, add the fresh tomatoes, sun-dried tomatoes with their oil, and parsley. Stir-fry one minute. Turn off the heat and add the goat cheese, stirring until it dissolves and melts into the sauce.

Return the scallops to the sauce pot and mix thoroughly. Keep sauce warm while the pasta finishes cooking, making sure that the sauce does not boil.

When pasta is cooked, drain, toss with the sauce, and serve.

79
Linguine with Scallops and Cauliflower
Linguine con Cannestrelli e Cavolfiore

Here is a wonderful autumnal dish reflecting a season when the scallops are fresh (if you live near the sea) and the cauliflower is ripe in the fields. We use bay scallops, but if you cannot find these, the larger sea scallops cut into quarters will do. If you prefer, broccoli may be substituted for cauliflower. Careful, broccoli needs less time to parboil than cauliflower does.

1 small cauliflower
½ cup (125 ml) olive oil
1 teaspoon crushed red pepper
1 lb (500 g) linguine
1 tablespoon (15 g) butter
2 cloves garlic, pressed or minced
l lb (500 g) bay scallops
¼ teaspoon oregano
¼ cup (30 g) Italian parsley, finely chopped

Place the cauliflower whole into a pot of cold salted water. Cover. Bring to a boil over high heat and continue cooking seven minutes at a rolling boil until the cauliflower is *al dente*. Remove with tongs or a slotted spoon. Do not pour out the water; you will be cooking the pasta in it. Cut the cauliflower into scallop-sized florets. You should have about 2 cups (375 g) of florets.

Heat the olive oil, minus 2 tablespoons, in a sauce pot with the red pepper. When the oil is sizzling, add the cauliflower. Quickly stir-fry one minute, lower the heat, add ¼ cup (60 ml) of water from the pasta pot, cover, and set to simmer slowly.

Begin to cook the pasta.

In a separate pan, melt the butter in the remaining 2 tablespoons of olive oil, add the garlic, and sauté briefly over medium heat. Add the scallops and oregano and sauté until scallops are firm, about two minutes.

Remove both cauliflower and scallops from the heat. Sprinkle in the parsley as you mix them together gently.

By now, the pasta should be ready. Drain and toss with the scallops and cauliflower.

Shrimp
Gamberoni

It's easy to find shrimp in most supermarket fish sections as well as in specialty seafood shops. The number of shrimp per pound (500 g) varies according to size, but generally will yield the following amounts: medium, 36 to 40; large, 16 to 20; jumbo, 10 to 15. You may use any size, but if you use the large or jumbo size, you will have to cut them in half or thirds for use in the following recipes.

The shrimp you buy will have their heads already removed. You will need to remove the shell and devein them.

Shrimp cook very quickly, usually no more than two minutes. They become bright pink when they are done.

80
Linguine with Spicy Shrimp
Gamberon fra' diavola

This flambé sauce should be devilishly hot, so use as much red pepper as you can take. The flambé is a challenge and a cheap thrill to first timers. A half-cup (125 ml) of wine will not flame up much. If you like a big flame, use "high octane"—¼ cup (60 ml) of cognac.

1 lb (500 g) linguine
⅓ cup (85 ml) olive oil
1½ teaspoons crushed red pepper
2 cloves garlic, pressed or minced
1 lb (500 g) shrimp, peeled and deveined
½ cup (125 ml) wine, white or red
1½ lb (750 g) tomatoes, peeled and finely chopped
6 large basil leaves
½ teaspoon dried oregano
1 tablespoon Italian parsley, finely chopped

When all the ingredients are prepared and the pasta is in the boiling water, put the oil in your saucepan with the pepper and garlic over high heat. Just as the garlic starts to brown, add the shrimp and sear quickly on all sides, stirring constantly, about a minute or less, or until they start to turn pink . Add the wine and light with a match in several places to flambé. When the flame goes out, or if you can't get it to light after ten seconds, add the tomatoes, basil, oregano, and parsley. Cook another minute at most, not longer or the shrimp will become tough.

Drain the linguine when it is slightly underdone. Toss with the sauce, stirring to mix well. Let sit on a warm range a few minutes to absorb the liquid in the sauce.

Variation: Lobster fra' diaviola is a big favorite. For luxury pasta, substitute a pound (500 g) of lobster meat, cut up, for the shrimp.

81
Fusilli with Shrimp and Feta Cheese
Pasta Alla Greca

This recipe was taught to us by our cousin Marty Penza, who learned it from a Greek countess when he was a guest at her villa in Crete. Marty does not kiss and tell but this dish suggests some of the earthy atmosphere of the affair: seafood and corkscrew noodles in a tangy pink sauce of goat cheese and ripe tomato. The resinous taste of chilled retsina is perfect to wash it down.

16 oz (500 g) canned peeled tomatoes, with the juice

¾ lb (375 g) feta cheese

1 teaspoon oregano

12 black Greek olives, pitted and sliced

juice of 1 large lemon

1 lb (500 g) fusilli

⅔ cup (170 ml) olive oil

4 cloves garlic, minced

1 lb (500 g) large shrimp, peeled, deveined, and cut in thirds

Strain the tomatoes, cut them in quarters, and put the juice in a large pan. Crumble the feta cheese into the juice, mashing down any thick lumps with a fork. Heat slowly, but don't let boil, stirring to homogenize the feta. When this is done, add the oregano, olives, half the lemon juice, and tomatoes. Keep warm over low heat.

Bring the pasta water to a boil and add the fusilli.

In another pan, heat the olive oil over high heat and lightly brown the garlic. Add the shrimp and stir until done, about two minutes. Add the other half of the lemon juice. Then add the tomato-olive mixture. Stir well and turn off the heat so as not to overcook the shrimp.

Undercook the pasta, drain, and toss with the sauce. Cover and let the pasta sit five minutes to absorb the excess liquid.

82

Rotelle with Shrimp, Broccoli, Sun-Dried Tomatoes, and Porcini

Rotelle Alla Rococo

This dish is a mouthful. The meatiness of the broccoli, the complexity of the sun-dried tomatoes, the delicacy of the shrimp, and the profuse, urbane country essence of the porcini mushrooms combine to put us in a high baroque frame of mind.

¾ oz (24 g) dried porcini mushrooms
½ lb (250 g) tomatoes, peeled and chopped
2 teaspoons (10 ml) lemon juice
1 lb (500 g) medium shrimp, peeled and deveined
½ cup (125 ml) olive oil
2 cloves garlic, minced
½ teaspoon crushed red pepper
¼ lb (125 g) oil-cured sun-dried tomatoes, coarsely chopped
2 cups (375 g) broccoli, steamed *al dente* and cut into small
   florets (see page 35)
¼ cup (30 g) chopped parsley
1 lb (500 g) rotelle

Rinse the mushrooms well to remove any sand or grit. Soak them in a bowl with the chopped fresh tomatoes and their juice at least twenty minutes. (Cut very large pieces of porcini to 1 inch (2.5 cm).)

Sprinkle the lemon juice on the cleaned shrimp.

Heat the olive oil with the garlic and pepper over high heat. As it starts to sizzle, add the fresh tomato and mushrooms and stir one minute. Still over high heat, add the sun-dried tomatoes, stirring another minute. Now add the broccoli, mix well, and cook one minute. Add the shrimp and reduce the heat to low, cover, and cook gently another minute, stirring occasionally. Add the chopped parsley and stir. Remove from the heat, but keep warm.

Meanwhile, cook the rotelle, drain, and toss with the sauce, mixing well.

83
Shrimp, Bean, and Penne Salad
Insalata di Gamberoni e Cannellini

Most of the preparation for this salad can be done ahead of time, leaving nothing to do but cook the pasta and add it to the marinating shrimp and beans shortly before you serve it.

Try to buy medium-sized shrimp so that you will get 36 to 40 per pound (500 g). Don't overcook, especially since the shrimp will be "cooking" in the marinade for some time.

> 1 lb (500 g) shrimp, shelled and deveined
> 1 cup (185 g) canned canellini beans, drained and rinsed
> 1 cup (185 g) fennel, slivered
> 10 to 12 Sicilian green olives, pitted and finely chopped
> ¼ cup (3 g) Italian parsley, finely chopped
> ½ teaspoon dried thyme
> ½ teaspoon dried oregano
> 1 lb (500 g) penne

Boil the shrimp forty-five seconds, or until they just turn pink.

Place all the ingredients except the penne in a bowl and prepare the following dressing:

> ⅓ cup (85 ml) lemon juice
> 2 cloves garlic, pressed or finely minced
> salt and freshly ground black pepper, to taste
> ⅔ cup (170 ml) olive oil

Place the lemon juice, garlic, salt, and pepper in a bowl. Using a fork, slowly whisk in the olive oil until well blended.

Pour the dressing over the shrimp mixture. Let marinate one hour. Stir occasionally.

Cook the penne until it is slightly underdone (it will continue to soften as it sits in the sauce). Drain and mix with the marinated shrimp mixture.

Let stand, stirring occasionally, thirty to forty-five minutes before serving.

Crab
Grancio

84
Linguine with Crabmeat, Black Olives, and Walnuts
Grancio Alla Gianni

We learned this recipe from Gianni Letizia when we were visiting
Sicily in 1982. It is simple to make and cooks very quickly. The only
problem is finding the right crabmeat. Good, fresh crabmeat should be
sweet and mild, never fishy. We have found Alaska king crab legs to be
the closest substitute to their Tyrrhenian cousins. If you use frozen
legs, buy them already out of the shells.
A word of warning: Under **no** circumstance use pasteurized crabmeat.
This will ruin both the taste and texture of this otherwise
delectable dish.

l lb (500 g) king crab legs, shelled and lightly shredded
2 tablespoons (30 ml) fresh lemon juice
½ teaspoon crushed red pepper
2 cloves garlic, pressed or finely minced
¾ cup (185 ml) olive oil
1 cup (185 g) chopped onion
¼ cup (45 g) shallots (spring onions), minced
¼ cup (60 ml) white wine
1 lb (500 g) linguine
½ cup (60 g) chopped walnuts
10 black Greek olives, pitted and chopped
¼ cup (30 g) parsley, finely chopped
1 teaspoon coarsely cracked black pepper

Pick over the crabmeat and remove any cartilage or shell. Sprinkle
with the lemon juice and set aside.
Set the pasta water to boil.
Sauté the red pepper and garlic in the olive oil over high heat, add the
onion and shallots, lower the heat to medium, and sauté until the onion
becomes transparent, about five minutes, stirring frequently.
Start cooking the pasta.

Add the white wine to the saucepan, then simmer and stir three minutes. Add the crabmeat, stir well to coat, then quickly add the chopped walnuts, olives, parsley, and black pepper. Stir over high heat one minute, cover, and keep warm.

When the linguine is ready, drain, toss with the crab mixture, and serve immediately.

Lobster
Aragosta

85
Fettuccine with Lobster in Light Marinara
Fettuccine con Aragosta

Pasta with lobster is no doubt more American than Italian, but since pasta goes splendidly with seafood of any kind, why not enjoy it with the ocean's sweetest bounty? We recommend that you start with cooked, shelled lobster meat, available for a price at most fine fish stores. When the chore of boiling live lobsters is eliminated, this dish is quick and easy to prepare, making it even more of a favorite. Its success relies on the delectability of the lobster rather than any intricacy of preparation. We like to keep the sauce to a minimum so that it doesn't overpower the delicacy of the meat. This recipe is a true luxury.

> 2 large cloves garlic, pressed or finely minced
> ½ teaspoon crushed red pepper
> ½ cup (125 ml) olive oil
> ¾ lb (375 g) tomatoes, peeled and chopped into small pieces
> A large bunch basil (½ lb/250 g) leaves only
> 1 cup (120 g) Italian parsley, loosely packed, stems removed
> 1 lb (500 g) lobster meat, cooked and cut into bite-sized
> pieces (you may want to save some larger pieces or the
> claws as a garnish)
> 1 lb (500 g) fettuccine

Heat the garlic and pepper in the olive oil until sizzling. Add the tomatoes. Stir over high heat thirty seconds. Add the basil and parsley and stir another thirty seconds. Add the lobster meat. Turn off heat immediately. Mix well.

Cook the fettuccine until tender. Drain, toss with the sauce, and serve. Garnish with the reserved lobster, if you wish.

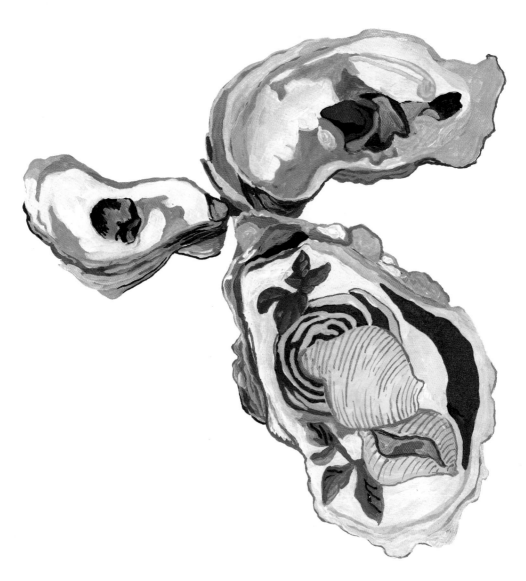

Oysters
Ostriche

86
Stuffed Shells Oysters, the "Gov"
Conchieglie Ripieni Ostriche Oreganata

In his latter years, Uncle Louie sold art rather than insurance. We do
not like to drop names, but one of his clients was "Caesar" himself,
"Zio" Nelson, the governor of a large industrial northeast state, and

Louie actually once had him over to the house on Fourth Avenue for Sunday dinner. Something special was in order. Aunt Celia, whose artistic impulses were channeled into cookery, created the following in honor of his honor. Here is her novel and classy version of a classic.

¼ lb (125 g) pancetta, thickly sliced then diced ¼ inch (5 mm)

¾ cup (180 ml) olive oil

¾ teaspoon crushed red pepper

2 lb (1 kg) watercress, stems removed, chopped

2 tablespoons pernod or anisette

1 cup (120 g) bread crumbs

½ cup (125 ml) lemon juice

⅓ cup (85 ml) olive oil

2 tablespoons dried oregano

1 lb (500 g) jumbo conchieglie (approximately 36)

1 lb (500 g) oysters, shucked (There should be one oyster per pasta shell. If the oysters are small, there should be enough. If they are large, cut them in half.)

Sauté the diced pancetta over high heat until crisp, about five to ten minutes. Remove from the pan and discard the fat.

Place the olive oil and red pepper in a pan over high heat and add the watercress a handful at a time, stirring constantly until it wilts and cooks down, about three minutes. Add the pernod and stir well one minute. Remove from the heat and place in a blender to grind coarsely. Put in a bowl, mix in the cooked pancetta, and set aside.

Mix together the bread crumbs, lemon juice, oil, and oregano.

Preheat the oven to 375° F (190° C/gas 5).

Boil the shells in salted water until they are just flexible enough to work with, six to eight minutes. Drain. Place one oyster and a spoon of the watercress mixture into each shell. Save the seasoned watercress liquid left in the bowl.

Place the shells, as you stuff them, in an oiled baking dish large enough to hold them all in one layer. When all are assembled, dribble with the seasoned watercress liquid. Spread the oregonata (oregano mixture) on top. Cover securely and bake twenty minutes. Remove the cover and place under a hot grill two or three minutes to brown, being careful not to burn the topping. Serve immediately.

Squid
Calamari

Squid, or *calamari*, is a big favorite in Sicily. Many of our American friends are unfamiliar with it and associate it with bait, something slimy. In fact, calamari is a quite firm and very mild-tasting fish, sweet with a somewhat chewy texture.

The body and the tentacles are the edible parts. The inky liquid is used to make pasta sauce as well as black pasta. Ordinarily, however, the ink is thrown away.

To clean squid, put your cutting board on the edge of the sink, lay the fish out flat, and with a sharp knife, remove the tentacles and set aside. A piece of the beak might still be lodged at the center of the tentacles. Push it out and discard. Cut off the rest of the head and discard. Take off the thin, speckled outer skin. It should simply peel off, taking the back fins with it. Discard these as well. Now put your finger into the wide opening of the body and run it along the inside edge until you feel a thin, clear piece of cartilage. It feels like plastic. This is the squid's backbone. Pull it out carefully. The insides should come out with it. Discard. You should have a white conical tube when you are finished. This is usually sliced into thin rounds.

Cleaning squid yourself is not all that difficult, but it can be messy, especially if you break the ink sac located just behind the head. Most fish markets will clean the squid for an extra dollar or two.

Whenever possible, we try to get small, young squid. These are usually the most tender.

87
Linguine with Squid and Peas
Linguine con calamari y piselli

Here is a spicy red sauce that is a favorite of ours.

1 clove garlic, pressed or finely minced

¾ teaspoon crushed red pepper

½ cup (125 ml) olive oil

1 lb (500 g) tomatoes, peeled and chopped

25 large basil leaves

¼ cup (30 g) Italian parsley, finely chopped

½ teaspoon dried oregano

6 oz (185 g) tomato paste

1 lb (500 g) linguine

2 lbs (1 kg) squid, cleaned and cut into thin rounds,
    tentacles cut individually, or 1lb (500 g) precleaned squid

1½ cups (280 g) baby peas, fresh or frozen

Heat the garlic and pepper in olive oil over high heat. Add the tomatoes, basil, parsley, and oregano and stir-fry sizzling hot one minute. Lower the heat, mix in the tomato paste, cover, and cook ten minutes at a slow simmer, stirring occasionally.

Bring the pasta water to a boil and add the linguine.

Add the cleaned and sliced squid to the sauce. Cook three to five minutes at a slow boil. Add the peas and turn off the heat immediately. Peas should be virtually raw.

If your sauce seems runny, undercook the pasta, drain, and let it sit with the sauce three to five minutes on the warm stove before serving.

149

88
Rotelle Salad with Squid, Fennel, and Orange
Insalata Calamari

This is a Sicilian-style squid salad, using oranges, and fennel instead of
celery. Rotelle is a wheel-shaped pasta, often called *wheels*. They come
in various lengths and widths. Many varieties have spokes. Try to find
the circular pasta closest to the squid in width. For a different, but
equally pleasing effect, you may use fusilli. In a pinch, rigatoni will do.
The following recipe, if made in the suggested proportions, will serve
more than four people. This is good party food because it should be
made beforehand and refrigerated before serving. Leftovers can be
saved and used the next day. If you have never eaten squid, this is a
good dish to try. If you are squeamish, or have guests that are, we
suggest you do not use the tentacles, only the rings. Use your visual
sense to cut the squid bodies in rounds that resemble the pasta,
remembering that when the pasta is cooked, it will be a bit larger than
it started, while the squid, after a couple of minutes in boiling water,
will shrink. Dressed, the two will look quite similar.
To clean squid, see page 148 for instructions. Remember: Be careful
not to break the ink sac.

2 cups (375 g) fennel hearts, finely minced
1 cup (185 g) purple onion, finely minced
½ cup (60 g) Italian parsley, finely minced
1 cup (250 ml) olive oil
juice of three lemons
4 lb (2 kg) squid, cleaned and cut into thin rounds,
   or 2 lb (1 kg) precleaned squid
1 lb (500 g) rotelle
¾ teaspoon crushed red pepper
3 seedless oranges, sectioned, sections cut in half
Boston lettuce, another soft lettuce, or endive leaves

Place the fennel, onion, and parsley in a large mixing bowl with the oil and the lemon juice.

Bring pasta water to a boil. Put the cleaned, sliced squid in a strainer or colander and immerse two minutes in the boiling water. Drain well and let cool.

Now boil the rotelle in the same pot. If you are going to let the salad sit in the refrigerator (we suggest you do), undercook the pasta since it will continue to soften as it absorbs the dressing. The end result should be firm.

While the pasta cooks, add the squid, pepper, and oranges to the mixing bowl and toss until they are well mixed.

When the pasta is ready, drain and add to the mixing bowl with the other ingredients. Toss.

Refrigerate at least one hour, longer if possible.

When ready to eat, turn the salad onto a platter lined with a bed of lettuce. Serve individual portions on lettuce or endive, making sure you garnish with the fine mincings and dressing which will inevitably sink to the bottom.

Swordfish
Pesce Spada

89
Rigatoni with Swordfish, Lemon, Anchovies, and Herbs
Rigatoni con Pesce Spada, Limone, Acciuge e Erba Aromatica

Although the list of ingredients may seem daunting, this is one of the easiest dishes to make. It is the marinade of aromatic herbs which gives it a complex flavor. The swordfish should marinate ahead of time then quickly cook while the pasta boils.

> 1 lb (500 g) swordfish, diced ½ inch (1 cm)
> ½ cup (125 ml) olive oil
> ¼ cup (60 ml) lemon juice
> 1 clove garlic, pressed or finely minced
> 1 tablespoon Italian parsley, chopped
> 1 teaspoon dried basil or 10 fresh basil leaves
> 1 teaspoon chives, minced
> ½ teaspoon oregano
> ½ teaspoon thyme
> ¼ teaspoon sage
> ¼ teaspoon rosemary
> 5 green olives, pitted and minced
> 5 anchovies, drained and mashed
> ¼ lb (125 g) tomatoes, peeled and chopped
> 1 lb (500 g) rigatoni
> ¼ teaspoon crushed red pepper

Combine all the ingredients except the crushed red pepper, pasta, and ¼ cup (60 ml) of the olive oil. Marinate one hour.

Bring the pasta water to a boil. Start cooking the rigatoni.

Heat the remaining ¼ cup (60 ml) of olive oil with the pepper in the sauce pot. When the oil is hot, add the marinated swordfish with the marinade and sauté over high heat for three to five minutes. Remove from direct heat, but keep warm.

When the rigatoni is done, drain and toss with the sauce.

Tuna
Tonno

Although canned tuna is acceptable in pasta dishes, now that fresh tuna is readily available, we strongly suggest you use it to escape that ordinary, everyday tuna salad flavor. If you are lazy, or live in an area where fresh fish is not available, by all means use canned, but use only good quality tuna packed in olive oil, which is almost always the imported variety. Not only does water and cheap vegetable oil leach the essential healthy oils from the tuna, our Uncle Mario told us he has heard rumors that dolphins and other mammals have turned up as filler canned with the fish. We assume that the rude individual who has the poor taste to dispose of business problems in this way could only sell the product to the cheapo brands, and not reputable Italian packing houses. We certainly wouldn't want somebody else's problem repeating on *us* in our bowl of macaroni.

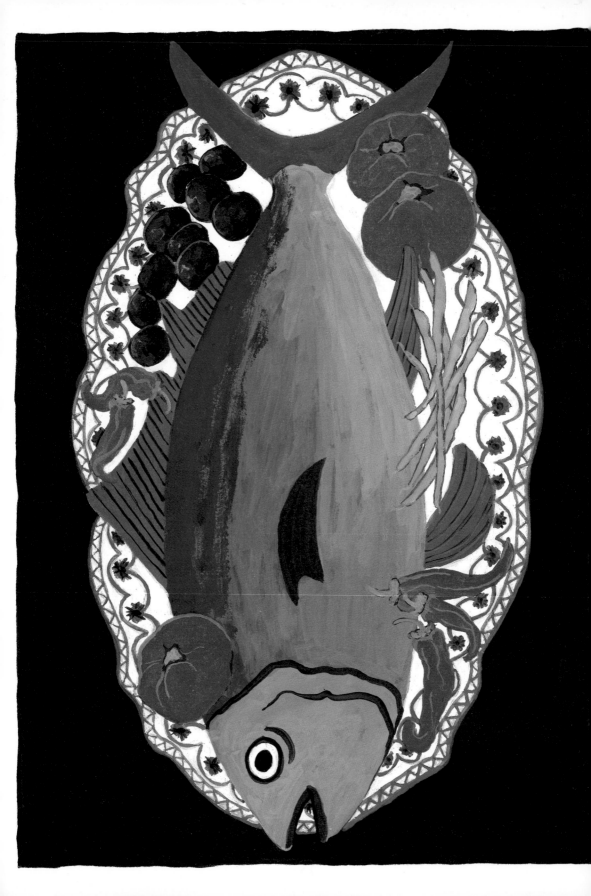

90
Linguine with Tuna, Black Olives, String Beans, and Capers
Linguine con Tonno

For several years, there was an effort to bring gambling to Montauk. Uncle Mario, hoping to get into the game, was spending a lot of time out there, enjoying the good life. He filled his days by going fishing on one of the charter boats. Prior to that, the only time Mario ever saw a fish was when it was breaded, fried, and laying on his plate, so nobody was more surprised than Mario the day he hooked a seventy-five-pound (35 kg) tuna. With all the stories of who might be sleeping with the fishes, he told us that he was more relieved than proud when his catch turned out to be 100 percent seafood.

1 lb (500 mg) linguine

1 clove garlic minced or pressed

¼ teaspoon crushed red pepper

½ cup (125 ml) olive oil

1 lb (500 g) tuna, cut into pieces ½ inch (1 cm),
    or 6 oz (185 g) canned tuna packed in olive oil, preferably imported Italian tuna, drained

¼ lb (125 g) French string beans, cut in thirds, parboiled two minutes

16 oil-cured black olives, pitted, finely chopped

2 tablespoons (30 ml) salt-cured capers

½ lb (250 g) tomato, peeled and chopped

2 tablespoons finely chopped parsley

2 tablespoons chopped chives

In this recipe, it's important for the pasta and the sauce to be done at the same time so that the fresh tuna does not continue to cook while it sits on the stove, so prepare and assemble the ingredients.

Start cooking the linguine, and when it is nearly tender, bring the garlic, pepper, and olive oil to a sizzle over high heat in your sauce pot. Add the tuna, searing evenly on all sides, then the remaining ingredients, stirring constantly over high heat, adding a tablespoon or two of the boiling pasta water. This should take **no longer than a minute!**

Drain the pasta, toss with the tuna sauce, and serve immediately.

Variation: For an especially fishy experience, add four mashed anchovies after you sear the tuna.

91

Shells with Tuna
Conchieglie Silicianiçoise

This dish shares a common ancestry with the French classic, *salad niçoise*. As the French forces who occupied the country in 1282 had to leave Sicily in a big hurry, the version they took had to be eaten cold, as a salad, minus, alas for them, the fundamental ingredient: the pasta.

¼ cup (60 ml) vinegar or lemon juice
1 tablespoon Dijon mustard
1 clove garlic, peeled
salt and pepper, to taste
¾ cup (185 ml) olive oil
1 lb (500 g) tuna, cut into pieces 1 inch (2.5 cm)
1 lb (500 g) new potatoes, peeled and diced
½ lb (250 g) string beans, cut in thirds
¾ lb (375 g) tomatoes, peeled and cut in eighths
4 anchovies, drained
10 black Greek olives, pitted and sliced
1 lb (500 g) conchieglie rigate
2 hard-boiled eggs, sliced

Place the vinegar, mustard, garlic, and salt and pepper in a blender or food processor. Blend at high speed thirty to forty seconds. Gradually pour the olive oil into the blender in a thin stream and blend until the ingredients are smooth. This will make one cup of vinaigrette. Any left over can be stored for up to three weeks in the refrigerator.

Marinate the tuna in the dressing thirty minutes.

Boil the potatoes until tender in the water in which you will cook the pasta, approximately five minutes. Remove with a slotted spoon. Boil the string beans in the same water four minutes and remove with the slotted spoon. Add the potatoes, string beans, tomatoes, anchovies, and olives to the tuna and dressing.

Let sit for at least thirty minutes. Place the marinade with the tuna and vegetables in a large saucepan. Bring to a boil over high heat. Stir well to mix and turn off the heat.

Cook the conchieglie until almost *al dente*, drain and return to the pot. Toss with the marinated tuna and vegetables and stir constantly over heat. If it seems too dry, add a spoonful or two more of the dressing while heating.

Add the sliced egg. Toss gently and serve immediately.

Salmon
Salmone

Needless to say, the Mediterranean is no great source of salmon. Nowadays, fresh salmon makes its way to southern Italy on ice, and Sicilian chefs prepare it as they would other meaty fish, with olives, herbs, and capers. But Sicilians have been acquainted with salmon since ancient times. Records dating back to the eighth century, from the Byzantine capital at Syracuse before it fell into the hands of the Arabs, show that Sicilian merchants traded with the Norwegians for smoked salmon, which was popular all across the island. Later, during the Spanish Inquisition, fleeing Sephardic Jews flocked to Sicily, reawakening a taste for the delicacy. Again, the history of a family can recapitulate the history of a people.

92
Penne with Salmon and Ricotta Salata
Penne con Salmone e Ricotta Salata

Many pasta dishes with salmon include the use of heavy or thick cream. We are convinced that not only is ricotta salata cheese easier to digest, it is also much tastier.

This recipe was given to us by our good friend Dominic Pastrini, a Palermo restaurateur. It has had a place on his menu for more than a decade. Dominic uses tarragon in spite of the fact that it shows some French influence. The Sicilians were never ones to throw the baby out with the bath water.

> 1 lb (500 g) salmon, filleted, skinned, and sliced in lengths ½ by 2 inches (1 by 5 cm)
> 1 teaspoon (5 ml) lemon juice
> 1 tablespoon (15 g) butter
> ½ cup (125 ml) olive oil
> 6 scallions, thinly sliced, or chopped chives
> 12 Sicilian green olives, pitted and finely chopped
> 2 tablespoons Italian parsley, chopped
> 1 teaspoon dried tarragon
> ¾ lb (375 g) asparagus (12 medium spears), steamed *al dente,* cut in thirds
> 1 lb (500 g) penne
> ¼ lb (125 g) ricotta salata cheese, coarsely crumbled

Toss the salmon strips in the lemon juice.

Melt the butter in the olive oil. Over high heat, sauté the scallions about one minute.

Add the salmon, stirring and turning gently to sear on all sides, about one minute. Add the olives, parsley, and tarragon and stir. Add the asparagus, stir well. Remove from direct heat, cover, and keep warm.

Cook the pasta. Drain and return to the pot. Add the ricotta salata and the salmon sauce, mixing all ingredients together over low heat. Serve.

Variations: A tablespoon of capers may be added.

Additional green olives add extra flavor.

Fresh ricotta may be substituted for ricotta salata for a milder taste. If so, do not toss with the other ingredients, but add a tablespoon to the top of each serving.

If good asparagus is not available, substitute ½ lb (250 g) of steamed string beans cut in thirds.

93
Smoked Salmon and Ricotta Lasagna
Lasagna di Matina

Aunt Isabelle used to make a lasagna dish with ricotta and anchovies. She was so crazy about the combination that she would usually keep fresh ricotta with anchovies mashed into it on hand in her refrigerator to use as a spread on bread or crackers. When, as kids, we used to go to her house to play with our cousins, Joey and Vinny, we would sneak vodka from Uncle Sal's big jug, listen to "Shout" by the Isley Brothers turned up full blast, and eat Aunt Isabelle's anchovy cheese spread on Fig Newtons. Years later, Joey married a mouthwatering dish named Carol Rosen. Carol made a big hit with her mother-in-law by introducing her to a toasted bagel with cream cheese and lox. Aunt Isabelle flipped. Great! Just like her ricotta and anchovies, but different.

After little Joey was born, Aunt Isabelle would always stop by on Sundays on her way home from Mass to visit her grandson, have coffee, and chew a few bagels with Carol. One Sunday in September, she brought over some tomatoes from her garden, and she and Carol got out the lasagna pan for a little experiment. We arrived later to watch the kickoff of the Jets game with Joey, and caught this marvelous dish just as it was coming out of the oven. A perfect brunch pasta, so mild-tasting you could eat it in your sleep.

To make one pound of lasagna you will need a baking dish that measures 8 by 10 by 3 inches (20 by 25 by 7 cm). Serves six to eight.

> 1 lb (500 g) lasagna
> ½ cup (125 ml) olive oil
> ½ cup (60 g) Italian parsley, finely chopped
> 1 tablespoon thyme
> 2 tablespoons chopped chives
> 1 lb (500 g) ricotta cheese
> ½ lb (250 g) smoked salmon (nova), thinly sliced (at least 8 slices)
> 2 lb (1 kg) tomatoes, thinly sliced

Preheat the oven to 375° F (190° C/gas 5).

Boil the lasagna in water to which you have added 1 tablespoon (15 ml) of the olive oil so that the lasagna doesn't stick. Cook until flexible, four to five minutes, remove from heat, pour out half the hot water, and add cold water to the pot to stop the noodles from cooking further.

In a bowl, mix ¼ cup (30 g) of the parsley, the thyme, chives, and ricotta.

Oil the baking dish. You will be laying down three layers of noodles, two layers of cheese, two of salmon, and three of tomatoes, so divide accordingly.

Place the first layer of noodles on the bottom of the baking dish. If you have an extra noodle or two, or broken noodle pieces, put them on the bottom or middle layer. Make sure that they overlap to make a firm foundation. Spoon half of the cheese-herb mixture on top, spreading evenly. A metal spoon dipped in a bowl of ice water will help you to spread the cheese gently without its sticking and making a mess of your noodle layer. Place a layer of half the smoked salmon slices on top of the cheese, then a layer of tomatoes on top of that. Dribble two tablespoons (30 ml) of olive oil on top of the tomatoes.

Place the second layer of noodles on top of this and layer with cheese, salmon, tomatoes, and olive oil.

Place the remaining third of the noodles on top. Spread with the remaining tomatoes, parsley, and oil. Cover tightly with aluminum foil.

Place in the oven and bake forty minutes. Remove the foil and bake uncovered an additional five minutes.

Remove from the oven and let stand at least twenty minutes or more before serving so that the layers will set.

Variation: If you're an anchovy lover, substitute three 2-oz (60 g) cans of anchovies, drained, for the smoked salmon. Put half on the bottom layer and the remaining half in the middle layer. The original recipe didn't use fresh tomatoes. Instead, Aunt Isabelle would ladle a big tablespoon of marinara sauce on the bottom and top only.

94
Linguine with Broccoli and Smoked Salmon
Linguine con Salmone Affumicato

Another creation of Isabelle Corsi and Carol Rosen Corsi.

> ¼ lb (125 g) smoked salmon, cut into strips 2 inches (5 cm)
> 1 tablespoon fresh lemon juice
> 2 cups (375 g) broccoli
> ½ cup (125 ml) olive oil
> ¼ teaspoon crushed red pepper
> ¼ cup (30 g) Italian parsley, chopped
> 1 lb (500 g) linguine

Place the smoked salmon in a dish, squeeze the lemon juice over it, and set aside.

Heat the pasta water. Parboil the broccoli in this pot, remove, and cut into small florets (see page 35).

Put the oil in your saucepan with the pepper over medium heat. When the pepper starts to sizzle, add the broccoli, stirring, and coat evenly about three minutes, still over medium heat. If the mixture seems too dry, add a tablespoon or two of water from the pasta pot at this time.

Add the salmon strips and chopped parsley and cook one minute longer to heat thoroughly.

Cook and drain the linguine and toss with the salmon-broccoli mixture. Serve immediately.

Sturgeon
Storione

Sturgeon is native to the temperate waters of the Northern Hemisphere and is fished from Scandinavia to the Mediterranean. Sicilians have long enjoyed it in numerous forms, especially since the arrival of the first Sephardim on their shores. It is prized as a symbol of longevity (some sturgeon live as long as 200 to 300 years) and fertility (probably due to the vast number of eggs they produce, which we know as caviar).

95

Linguine with Smoked Sturgeon, Arugula, and Shiitake Mushrooms
Linguine Epicureo

Smoked sturgeon resurfaced in our family as a result of one of cousin Vinny's many visits to Miami Beach to visit his brother Joey and his wife, Carol. It was there he met, romanced, and became engaged to the princesslike Stefanie Kellerman. We were familiar with smoked sturgeon, but when Stefanie's mom, the indomitable Bella, announced her plan to serve "a nice sturgeon plate" as a first course at the wedding reception, hell broke loose in the family. We were willing to turn the other cheek when they told us they were getting married by a rabbi; but no macaroni? How would we explain this ethnic lapse of menu protocol to the more distant family members and business associates?

Aunt Isabelle and Cousin Carol came to the rescue. Working with Frank Napoli of Epicurean Foods, whom Bella had hired to cater the reception, they invented a new dish using ingredients that did justice to both cultures, honoring bride and groom. And just to show that their *nouvelle*-found tolerance knew no bounds, they added *fungi Giaponese* to the melting pot. The following recipe is the result of that happy union.

> ¼ lb (125 g) sliced smoked sturgeon, julienned
>
> 2 tablespoons (30 ml) lemon juice
>
> 2 tablespoons (30 g) sweet butter
>
> ½ cup (125 ml) olive oil
>
> ½ lb (250 g) shiitake mushrooms, tough stems removed, julienned
>
> ¼ teaspoon crushed red pepper
>
> 1 bunch arugula, finely sliced (6 oz/185 g)
>
> 1 lb (500 g) linguine

Place the sturgeon strips in a bowl and sprinkle with the lemon juice.

Heat the butter and ¼ cup (60 ml) of the olive oil in your saucepan. Add the mushrooms and stir-fry quickly over high heat until soft, approximately two minutes. Remove. Place in a bowl and set aside.

Add the remaining ¼ cup (60 ml) of olive oil and the crushed red pepper to the saucepan. When the oil is hot, toss in the arugula, and sizzle and stir over high heat until wilted. Turn off the heat.

Add the sautéed shiitake mushrooms and the sturgeon to the cooked arugula. Keep warm.

Cook the pasta, drain, and toss with the sturgeon, mushroom, and arugula. Mix well, but gently!

Caviar
Caviale

Caviar is the common name for fish eggs preserved in salt. When the roe comes from sturgeon, it can be quite costly, but we find that the ordinary, widely available and popularly priced red salmon caviar works well with pasta. Beware of cheap varieties that try to imitate the real thing. They tend to have a gritty feel on the palate and an unpleasant aftertaste. We have never used expensive beluga or sevruga caviar in this recipe, so we are not sure that they would be better. In any case, this is a luxury sauce, not for those who have no taste for caviar.

96
Spaghettini with Caviar, Potatoes, and Ricotta
Pasta al caviale, con patates e ricotta

While this dish is stylish, it is by no means *nuovo*. Legend tells us that in 1849, Pope Pius IX served it to the Duke of Ragusa at a party in Rome honoring him for his great humility in service to the Church.

> 10 oz (315 g) new potatoes, peeled
> ¼ teaspoon crushed red pepper
> ½ cup (125 ml) olive oil
> ½ cup (60 g) chives, finely chopped
> ½ cup (60 g) Italian parsley, finely chopped
> 1 teaspoon freshly ground black pepper
> 1 lb (500 g) spaghettini
> 4 oz (125 g) red salmon caviar, sprinkled with lemon juice
> fresh ricotta cheese

Boil the potatoes in water to cover until tender, and dice into 1-inch (2.5-cm) pieces. Save a ¼ cup (60 ml) of the potato water for the sauce. The rest can be added to the pasta water.

Heat the red pepper in the oil. When the pepper starts to sizzle, add the chives and parsley, and mix thirty seconds over medium-high heat. Add the potatoes and mix quickly, adding two or more spoons of reserved water to keep the mixture from sticking to the pot. Sprinkle with the black pepper. Remove from the heat, but keep warm.

Cool the pasta, drain, and toss with potato-chive mixture. Now add the caviar and toss gently. Caviar should get warm but not cook, except a bit from the heat of the warm spaghetti. No hard-boiled fish eggs!

Serve with a tablespoon of fresh ricotta cheese on top of each portion.

Mixed Seafood
Frutta di Mare

97
Acini di Pepe, Sicilian Style, with Seafood and Garden Vegetables
Acini di Pepe, Marinaro e Giardino

Acini di pepe is similar to couscous but will not cook as quickly. Therefore, it is necessary to parboil the acini before adding it to the other ingredients. Don't let the long list of ingredients intimidate you. This recipe will serve six to ten people, depending on what else you serve with it. We call for 2 pounds (1 kg) of mixed seafood. You can make seafood and vegetable substitutions according to your taste or depending on what is available. You'll need a large skillet with a cover.

2 lb (1 kg) acini di pepe
¾ cup (180 ml) olive oil
2 tablespoons (30 g) butter
2 large cloves garlic, pressed or finely minced
1 teaspoon crushed red pepper
1 cup (185 g) onion, chopped
2 cups (375 g) zucchini, cubed
½ cup (90 g) diced carrot
½ cup (90 g) diced celery
2 lbs (1 kg) tomatoes, peeled and chopped
6 anchovies, drained
¼ cup (30 g) Italian parsley, finely chopped
1 teaspoon cumin
¼ teaspoon sage
1 cup (250 ml) clam juice, or 10 oz (315 g) canned baby
  clams with the juice
1 cup (250 ml) white wine
½ lb (250 g) swordfish, diced ½-inch (1 cm)
½ lb (250 g) medium shrimp (approximately twenty), shelled
  and deveined
½ lb (250 g) bay scallops (or ocean scallops, quartered)
½ lb (250 g) cleaned calamari, cut into rounds
1½ cups (375 g) baby peas, fresh or frozen

As in recipe 70 (page 123), parboil the acini di pepe in 6 quarts (6 liters) of salted water three minutes. Strain. Place in a ceramic bowl, mixing it thoroughly with ¼ cup (60 ml) of the olive oil. Cover with a plate until you are ready to use.

Heat the butter in the remaining ½ cup (125 ml) of olive oil in the large skillet. Add the garlic, pepper, and onion. Sauté five minutes over medium heat. Add zucchini, carrots, celery. Sauté three minutes.

Add the tomatoes, anchovies, parsley, cumin, and sage and sauté three more minutes. Add the clam juice and wine, bring to a boil, and lower heat.

Add the acini, spreading it evenly over the vegetable stew. Do not stir it in. You may have to break up clumps with your hands. Arrange the seafood attractively on top of the layer of acini, add the peas, and cover.

Simmer slowly about forty-five minutes, or until the seafood is steamed through and the acini is tender. If you need to add additional liquid, we recommend having another bottle of clam juice on hand, or, if you use canned tomatoes, save the juice and use it. When the dish is done, all the liquid should be absorbed by the acini.

98
Penne Paella
Penne Spagnuolo

In this otherwise classic version of the Spanish favorite, we use penne instead of the traditional rice. Of course, you could use riso or orzo, but the thin tubular macaroni makes it more of an adventure. Since the entire dish should be cooked in one pan and brought to the table, use a large, heavy pan with a cover. The following recipe will serve eight. As in the previous recipe, if any of the seafood is unavailable or not to your taste, feel free to improvise. Just make sure you get the same weight.

4 chicken thighs, halved
¼ cup (60 ml) balsamic vinegar
1 tablespoon (1g) butter
½ cup (125 ml) olive oil
2 cups (375 g) onion, chopped
2 cloves garlic, minced
1 teaspoon crushed red pepper
2 lb (1 kg) penne
1 lb (500 g) tomatoes, peeled and chopped
½ cup (60 g) Italian parsley, chopped
pinch saffron
2 hot sausages (8 oz/250 g), cooked and sliced (see page 101)
1 cup (250 ml) clam juice
½ cup (125 ml) white wine
1 cup (185 g) baby peas, fresh or frozen
½ lb (250 g) bay scallops, whole, or ocean scallops, quartered
½ lb (250 g) shrimp (about 20), peeled and deveined
½ lb (250 g) swordfish, diced 1 inch (2.5 cm)
1 lb (500 g) littleneck clams, washed, in their shells
12 (1 lb/500 g) mussels, washed, beards removed, in their shells

Marinate the chicken in the vinegar two hours. Assemble all the ingredients and bring the pasta water to a low boil.

Melt the butter in the olive oil, add the onion, garlic, and red pepper and sauté over high heat five minutes, stirring constantly.

Add the chicken and braise it, turning often to brown evenly, five to ten minutes. Remove from saucepan and set aside.

Boil the penne four minutes or less. Drain. Place in the saucepan with the chopped tomatoes and parsley. Sprinkle with the saffron and stir over low heat.

Return the chicken pieces to the pan and add the sausage rounds. Toss well.

Add the clam juice and the white wine, mix well.

Place the peas and seafood on top, arranged in a decorative pattern. Cover and cook slowly over low heat twenty-five to thirty minutes. If it gets dry, add a little wine, clam juice, or tomato juice, but do be sparing. In the end, all the liquid should be absorbed, the penne should be *al dente*, the clams and mussels should be open, firm but tender, and the other fish and the meats slowly steamed done.

Serve immediately, making sure everyone gets a good sample of everything. (Remember to set a big bowl on the table for the shells and bones!)

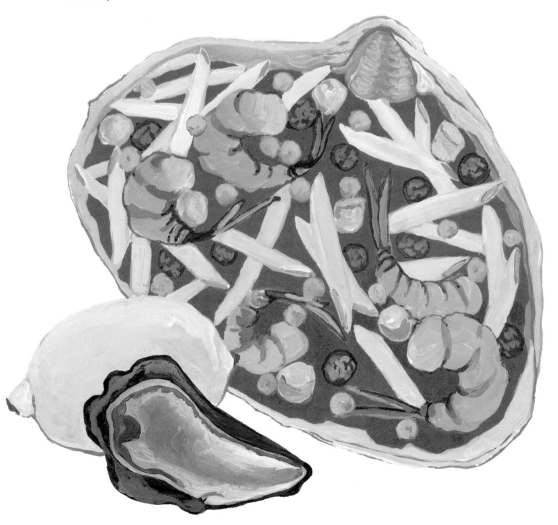

99
Seafood Lasagna
Lasagna al Frutta di Mare

Even today, the older family members still balk when someone marries
out of the clan, but when the outsider is French, the family practically
goes into mourning. It was a testament to cousin Pauline's willful ways,
as well as her culinary ability, that the first time she invited us to her
house for dinner after marrying Francois, she served us fish and
fromage in the same recipe. Though the Corsis have long eschewed the
mixing of seafood with cheese, this dish was so classy that we
swallowed our pride along with the *lasagna al frutta di mare*.
As for the type of goat cheese, any will do, but we recommend
Montrachet. This dish will serve six to eight.

1 lb (500 g) ricotta cheese
½ lb (250 g) goat cheese
1 egg
½ cup (125 ml) olive oil
¾ teaspoon crushed red pepper
1 clove garlic, pressed
1½ lb (750 kg) tomatoes, peeled and chopped
25 basil leaves
½ cup (60 g) parsley, finely chopped
¼ cup (45 g) fennel, finely chopped
1 tablespoon thyme
1 teaspoon oregano
2 bay leaves
½ lb (250 g) shrimp, peeled, deveined, and cut in half
    lengthwise
½ lb (250 g) scallops, cut in thirds
½ lb (250 g) lobster meat, thinly sliced
½ lb (250 g) salmon fillet, thinly sliced
1 lb (500 g) lasagna

Preheat the oven to 375°F (190°C/gas 5).

Mix the ricotta and goat cheese together with the egg.

Heat the olive oil, red pepper, and garlic. Add the tomatoes and herbs. Stir-fry two minutes over medium-high heat. Turn off the heat and remove the bay leaves. Add the seafood. Stir well and cover. Remove from the heat.

Drop the lasagna noodles into boiling water and cook until they become flexible enough to work with, four to five minutes. Remove from the heat, drain, and add cold water to stop the cooking.

Lightly oil baking pan measuring 8 by 10 by 3 inches (20 by 25 by 7 cm). Place a few teaspoons of the tomato sauce on the bottom (just enough so that the noodles don't stick). Place one third of the noodles on the bottom, overlapping slightly for a firm foundation. Dot the lasagna with half of the ricotta mixture, and spread evenly. Using a slotted spoon, place half of the seafood on top of the ricotta mixture. Distribute evenly.

Repeat the process with another third of the noodles, the rest of the ricotta mixture, the seafood (again using a slotted spoon), and the remaining lasagna noodles.

Spoon the remaining tomato sauce on top of the lasagna. Cover tightly and bake one hour. Remove the lasagna from the oven and let it settle for thirty minutes before serving.

John Penza and **Tony Corsi,** third-generation Sicilian Americans, are cousins, and combined, have over fifty-five years experience working as chefs in Brooklyn, Staten Island, and New Jersey. They visit and dine in Sicily regularly.

Miriam Dougenis, an award-winning artist, has exhibited her work extensively on Long Island, in New York City, and nationwide. She shows at Gallery East, East Hampton, N.Y.; Goat Alley Gallery, Sag Harbor, N.Y.; and Robert Kidd Gallery, Birmingham, Michigan. Currently, she teaches art at Guild Hall, East Hampton, N.Y., and the Islip Art Museum, East Islip, N.Y.